AWE WITH WORDS

Young Writers' 16th Annual Poetry Competition

It is feeling and force of imagination that make us eloquent.

How can I not dream while writing? The blank page gives a right to dream.

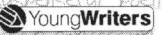

Inspirations From Scotland & Ireland

Edited by Allison Jones

First published in Great Britain in 2007 by:
Young Writers
Remus House
Coltsfoot Drive
Peterborough
PE2 9JX
Telephone: 01733 890066
Website: www.youngwriters.co.uk

All Rights Reserved

© Copyright Contributors 2007

SB ISBN 978-1 84431 240 2

Foreword

This year, the Young Writers' *Away With Words* competition proudly presents a showcase of the best poetic talent selected from thousands of up-and-coming writers nationwide.

Young Writers was established in 1991 to promote the reading and writing of poetry within schools and to the young of today. Our books nurture and inspire confidence in the ability of young writers and provide a snapshot of poems written in schools and at home by budding poets of the future.

The thought, effort, imagination and hard work put into each poem impressed us all and the task of selecting poems was a difficult but nevertheless enjoyable experience.

We hope you are as pleased as we are with the final selection and that you and your family continue to be entertained with *Away With Words Inspirations From Scotland & Ireland* for many years to come.

Contents

Craig Blackwood (13) — 1

Airdrie Academy, Airdrie
Pamela Buchanan (14) — 2
Kirstie McGlade (14) — 3
Laura Higgins (13) — 4
Chris Spiers (14) — 5
Fraser McKane (13) — 6
Fiona Barrie (13) — 7
Heather Richards (13) — 8
Justine McGrinder (14) — 9
Alana Neeson (14) — 10
Katie Sharp (13) — 11
Fraser Bell (14) — 12
Joanne Sefton (14) — 13
Rachel Gibb (13) — 14
Eva Kwok (14) — 15
Rachel Balmer (13) — 16
Emma Lowe (14) — 17
Laura Hopton (14) — 18

Auchinleck Academy, Auchinleck
Lex Sharpe (13) — 19

Aughnacloy College, Aughnacloy
Sophie Hall (14) — 20
Alison Campbell (14) — 21
Hannah Crawford (14) — 22
Joy Coote (14) — 23
Stewart McAlister (14) — 24
Karen Murphy (14) — 25
Shareen McMaster (14) — 26
Philip Caddoo (14) — 27
Gillian Brush (14) — 28
Sarah Morrow (14) — 29

Banchory Academy, Banchory
  Robert McClymont (14) — 30
  Marie Ewen (14) — 31

Bearsden Academy, Bearsden
  Mathew Miller (13) — 32
  Alexander Hendry (12) — 34
  Ranjeev Panesar (13) — 35
  Craig Wallace (14) — 36
  Adam MacLeod (12) — 37
  Amy Thomson (13) — 38
  Stephen Dickie (12) — 39
  Rebekah Hemming (13) — 40
  Dayle Hassan (13) — 41
  Caitlin Ord (12) — 42
  Caitlin Doyle (12) — 43
  Louise McCormick (12) — 44
  Fiona Byrne (12) — 45
  Anna Higgins (12) — 46
  Caitlin Chalmers (13) — 47
  Holly Shearer (12) — 48
  Jade Ellen Sturrock (12) — 49
  Sophie Wayt (13) — 50
  Holly Munn (14) — 51

Bellshill Academy, Bellshill
  Rhonda Stewart (12) — 52
  Nikki Tobin (12) — 53
  Jack Paton, Edwin Lau (12) & Callum Bulloch (13) — 54
  Richard Lovell & Joshua Abraham (12) — 55
  Marc Rodgers & Robbie McCrone (13) — 56
  Debi Gardiner (12) — 57
  Caroline Hassan (14) — 58
  Elliot Shepka (12) — 59
  Gemma McLean & Rachel Stewart (13) — 60
  Andrew Baxter (12) — 61
  Kelsey Caldwell & Nadia Murphy (12) — 62

Boclair Academy, Bearsden
  Cara Jane Kingsley (13) — 63

Cathkin High School, Cambuslang

Amy Rooney (13)	64
Stephanie Morrison (12)	65
Nicole Mulrooney (12)	66
Chloe Wellington (12)	67
Lauren Newbigging (12)	68
Lauren Campbell (12)	69
Andrew Law (13)	70
Dale Gray-Gardner (13)	71
Beth Cochrane (12)	72
Sharie Boyd (13)	73
Stephen Ponsonby (13)	74

Cedarbank School, Livingston

Ross Innes (15)	75
Harley Goldie (15)	76

Christian Brothers Secondary School, Belfast

James McQuade (14)	77
Michael Monaghan (14)	78
Corey Hamill (14)	79
Tony McNeilly (14)	80
Jonathan Copeland (14)	81
Seamus O'Doherty (14)	82
Mark Murtagh (16)	83
Patrick McCorry (16)	84
Stephen Wylie (15)	85

Drumglass High School, Dungannon

Amy Robinson (13)	86

Forfar Academy, Forfar

Chimene Samson (13)	87
Becca Fletcher (14)	88
Eilidh McMinn (14)	89
Rachel Findlay (14)	90
Christina Ilia (14)	91

Glencryan School (SEN), Cumbernauld

Robert Jardine (14)	92

Robert David Morrison Wright (13) — 93
William Walker (14) — 94
Scott Forsyth (13) — 95

Hamilton Grammar School, Hamilton
Heather Sinclair (13) — 96
Kelly Macnaught (13) — 97
Eilidh Laird (13) — 98
Vanessa McEwan (13) — 99
Ross Malley — 100

Harberton School, Belfast
Cáragh Cassidy (13) — 101

Hermitage Academy, Helensburgh
Kristina Hopps (15) — 102
Pamela Ross (12) — 103
Aimee MacPhail (12) — 104
Mollie Sheard (12) — 105
Luke Smith (12) — 106
Catriona Dolan (13) — 107
Mhairi Hanlon (12) — 108
Lauren Carruthers (12) — 109
Nadine Royle (13) — 110
Brad Lamington (13) — 111
Rebecca Watson (12) — 112
Kirsty Pristaw (12) — 113
Ella Mackay (12) — 114
Harry Crumless (12) — 115
Rosemary Jennings-Maun (12) — 116
David Pellow (14) — 117
Sophie Finn (12) — 118
David Reid (12) — 119
Alison West (12) — 120
Sarah Bonthrone (12) — 121
Callum Downs (12) — 122
Laura McGhie (13) — 123
Jasna Wardle (13) — 124
Atif Riaz (15) — 125
Gillian Allan (13) — 126
Christine McKelvie (14) — 127

Ashleigh Milnes (13)	128
Rosanagh Watson (15)	129
Simon Anderson (15)	130
Amy Thomas (14)	131
Sam Stacey (14)	132
Struan Wylie (12)	133
Megan Macaulay (14)	134
Holly Muir (12)	135
Stephanie Carpenter (12)	136
Carly Trille (12)	137
Rebecca Hamer (12)	138
Harry Cotton (12)	139
Frank Mulholland (13)	140

Islay High School, Bowmore

Ross Cameron (13)	141
Lucy Darroch (13)	142
Anna Storrie (14)	143

Knockevin Special School, Downpatrick

Kerry Gibson (19)	144
Lisa Stewart (16)	145
Charlene Anderson (19)	146
Clare Orr (18)	147
Ruairi Armstrong (18)	148

Our Lady of Mercy Girls' School, Belfast

Shannon Lawlor (12)	149

St Saviour's High School, Dundee

Connor Barrass (13)	150
Amy Miller (13)	151
Rebekah Sommerville (13)	152
Amber McIver (13)	153
Ciara McCluskey (14)	154
Demi-Louise Simpson (14)	155
Lee Gillespie (14)	156
Kelly Hunter (14)	157
James Mitchell (13)	158
Darlene Paxton (13)	159

Shimna Integrated College, Newcastle
Suzannah Dunn (14) 160
Nina Graham (13) 161
Elaine Kelly (14) 162
Kathryn Curry (14) 163
Gordon Donaldson (14) 164
David Mawhirt (14) 165
Kirsty Smyth (14) 166
Jane McEvoy (13) 167
Matt Boyle (14) 168
John Nellis (13) 169
Brian Nelson (14) 170
Naill McAnallen (14) 171

Stonelaw High School, Rutherglen
Ryan McCallum (14) 172
Julie Smith (13) 173

The Kibble School, Paisley
Jordan King (15) 174

Victoria College, Belfast
Vanessa Ifediora (17) 175
Shannon Magnano (14) 176
Nicola Woods (17) 177
Emma Lui (17) 178

Wellington School, Ayr
Kieran Gibson (12) 179
Rhona Ford (12) 180
Erin Corbett (12) 181
Robert Alner (13) 182
Oliver Greenall (12) 183
Colin Casey (13) 184
Sophie Durnan (13) 185
Rónán Hunter Blair (12) 186
Ruth Dunsmuir (12) 187
Rachel Doyle (13) 188
Sarah Rowan 189

Whitburn Academy, Whitburn
Robyn Bonnar (12) 190
Alanna Rolland (12) 191
Danielle Hunter (12) 192
Dianne Hughes (13) 193
Ryan Whyte (12) 194
Robbie Fairley (13) 195

The Poems

My Gran

My gran's my mum's mum.
My mum's her daughter.
She's a harmless wee soul; not a bad bone in her.
Let me tell you, last week she had a fly
In her house; it was not to die.
It got whacked out the window -
Lucky wee beastie -
If I saw it, it wouldn't stand a chance.
I hate them, don't you?

My gran's a perfectionist,
A Kim 'n' Aggie in disguise,
She's a shopaholic,
Her favourite one's Mackay's.
Got about thirty jackets, bought one last week,
Same with trousers, shoes and blouses,
I had a peek.
All clothes colour coordinated, like a rainbow in the sky -
Not like mine, it's a pure pig's sty!
She can text faster than me
And every day she murders five cups of tea.

Aw, her baking, it's really just the best -
She makes sponges and all the rest.

She is my pillow, just after it's washed.

A hooveraholic, we call her 'Noo Noo'
She really can't deal with sickness or poo.
She's so caring, a kind wee lady,
My gran hasn't got a car,
But keeps us all happy at home
And that's what grans are for!

Craig Blackwood (13)

One To Watch

She is like a chocolate cake,
Good in moderation.
She is pretty like the colour pink,
But only when she's asleep.
She is like a piccolo,
High-pitched and thin.
She is like a thistle,
Sharp and painful.
She is like an old rusty car,
Reliable but embarrassing.
She is like a sneaky monkey,
You never know what she'll do next.
She is like a ringbinder,
That could snap back any second.
She is like a cold winter's day,
It never seems to go away.
She is like a maths period,
Boring and confusing.

Pamela Buchanan (14)
Airdrie Academy, Airdrie

Dedication To Jennifer

She is fun like a new toy,
She is funny like a comedian,
She is warm like a summer's day,
But sometimes cold like snow in winter.
She talks a lot like a broken record!
And she's sometimes annoying
Like when it rains and you want sun,
But she's really caring, like a mother hen
And that's why she's my best friend.

Kirstie McGlade (14)
Airdrie Academy, Airdrie

She Is . . .

She is blue, cool and calm
She is apples, sweet tasting
She is Coke, fizzy and full of energy
She is ice skating, graceful and flawless
She is a sofa, comforting and relaxing
She is a daffodil, bright and sweet smelling
She is a flute, soft sounding and calming
She is a TV, entertaining and funny
She is number one.

Laura Higgins (13)
Airdrie Academy, Airdrie

The Pattern Of Life

Through all the ages,
There has been a pattern,
A pattern of life.
When life begins, a child is happy and carefree,
It is most dependent on its mother, its main guardian,
Who will always be there to protect.
As we get older, we have small issues to deal with -
The beginning of nursery,
Then school as we start to make our friends.
Then we start to push away,
To be rebellious, to stop listening,
Because we think we are right and everyone else is wrong.
Responsibilities come as we struggle
To pass the tests for our futures.
We start life of adulthood, the real one,
Where we have to make sensible choices
And leave home to make a life of our own.
As this time goes on, the little changes happen
That we need to stand back, to notice.
They add up to a bigger change,
These changes will keep happening
Until we face the biggest challenge.
Death.
Some people fear it, others welcome it,
But whether we want it or not, it is inevitable.

Chris Spiers (14)
Airdrie Academy, Airdrie

The One I Like

She is my sun in the day,
She brightens my way.
She is my stars at night,
Shining so bright.
She is my scarf in winter,
Comforts me from the cold.
She is my drink in the summer,
Keeps me cool and refreshed.
She is my gel for my hair,
Something I can't do without.
She is my mints in my pocket,
Great to have around.
She is my childhood doll,
A friend for life.
My good friend, someone,
The one I like.

Fraser McKane (13)
Airdrie Academy, Airdrie

All Alone

Without you I'm lonely,
I miss you all the time,
But when you're with me,
You are all mine.

But be aware,
Love is not everything,
Yet . . . there's something about it,
That makes me sing.

But remember, it could be alright,
Not everything goes wrong,
Don't let love lose your sight.

Fiona Barrie (13)
Airdrie Academy, Airdrie

Here To You, My Dear

Here to you, my dear
You occupy my heart
You will stay in my heart
Until we fade into the earth.

You will still be in my spirit
Until my spirit gets broken
But still I will look over you
Keep you safe
And lead you on to the correct paths of life.

You'll never have an empty heart
I will stay there to comfort you
When you are down or stressed.

I hope you will never replace me, my love . . .

Heather Richards (13)
Airdrie Academy, Airdrie

I Lost My Love

I stand alone in a crowded city
No one seems to take much pity
I lost my love to another man
She was gone, quicker than a passing van
My heart is broken, but on the mend
Just barely hanging on its end
I feel like there is still hope
But without my love, how can I cope?
For her hair, as fair as fair can be
Her face, ever so lovely
Her eyes, twinkle as the moonlight glows
Only when I see her, my love truly shows
Forever she will stay in my heart
Even though we are apart.

Justine McGrinder (14)
Airdrie Academy, Airdrie

A Poem Of Heartbreak

Love
Love is a fickle thing,
Love can be true - love can be false
And even though you can love,
Sometimes . . . you love me not.

You go to someone else
And I know that you love them,
So go away! Leave me be!
I don't want to be steeped in misery.

I'll find someone else that loves
And I'll love them more than you,
I'll find my true love, soon, you'll see
And for all I care - you can die of love.

Because you love *me* not.

Alana Neeson (14)
Airdrie Academy, Airdrie

Inside . . .
(Dedicated to my niece, Stephanie)

I look into my mirror
And what do I see?
A little girl with a heart of gold
Staring back at me.

I wish I were inside out
And people didn't have to be told.
I may laugh and smile as normal
But inside, I'm freezing cold.

I know that people think I'm strange
I know that they all stare.
My heart is dying with envy -
It's really so unfair.

Now, as I sit here in my chair
With family all about.
I smile and hold my head up high
If I'm sad, you won't find out.

Life is good, I can live
To tell a story still.
The things that I have gone through
Though, a dozen books they'd fill.

I'm really sweet and kind
But I'm disabled too.
And there's something everyone must learn -
I'm a child
Just like you.

Katie Sharp (13)
Airdrie Academy, Airdrie

Hate

He is a rusted old car
                Takes too long to start
He is an old, old turtle
                Very slow to do anything
He is a squeaky wheel
                Irritating at every turn
He is a rotten tooth
                Sore, painful and not wanted
He is rain
                Boring to watch and no fun
He is a dark cloud
                I'm miserable when around him
He is weak tea
                Boring and untasteful
He is a bass
                Droning and annoying
He is a hurricane
                Destructive and scary
I hate him.

Fraser Bell (14)
Airdrie Academy, Airdrie

If . . .

If she were a colour, she would be green
Sinful and envious, she's awful mean.
If she were make-up, she would be over-done,
Or bright orange just like the sun.
If she were a character, she'd be Cruella De Vil,
Sneaky, conniving, menacing and evil.
If she were an animal, she would be a kangaroo,
Too energetic, she should be kept in a zoo.
If she were a mythical creature, she would be a witch,
Mischievous and cunning, with devious tricks.
If she were the weather, she would be a hurricane,
Pushy and angry, she can be a pain.
If she were a conversation, she would be a murmur,
Quiet and secretive, oh, I hate her!

Joanne Sefton (14)
Airdrie Academy, Airdrie

The One, The Only
(For Rebecca Gibb)

The one,
She is the happy fairy tale,
Which can turn into a horror story.
She is icy blue, like the morning frost
And can change to agile amber.
She can be that stylish dress,
Or that old, itchy, knitted jumper.
She can be a solid suit of armour,
Or a sweet princess dress.
She could be a soft dolly shoe,
Or that painful stiletto you just can't wait to take off.
She is the cute cat in your garden
Who can all of a sudden, grab you like a lion.
She is like a brutal game of rugby
Or that beautiful ballet dance, when she wants to be.
It would look as if butter wouldn't melt in her mouth
But inside, she is a fudge cake, naughty yet nice!

Rachel Gibb (13)
Airdrie Academy, Airdrie

Person I Loathe

She is green, filled with jealousy,
She is like Coke, bad for you,
She is like a lemon, always leaves you feeling sour,
She is a pair of smelly socks, best avoided,
She is a pair of high heels, hard and uncomfortable,
She is like a tuba, low and dull,
She is a monkey, always giving you cheek,
She is geography, bores you to death,
She is autumn, where everything dies,
She is like a long fringe, always in your way,
She is like foundation, hides up everything,
She is a simulated gem, cheap and fake,
I hate her!

Eva Kwok (14)
Airdrie Academy, Airdrie

My Best Friend

She is like a chrysanthemum,
Closing up to who she does not please,
Then flourishing for those she loves.
She is like a flute,
Playing a gorgeous concerto,
While being greatly admired.
She is like a guide dog,
When I stray off the path,
She leads me back
And is only too happy to stay by my side.
If she were the weather,
She would be the snow,
You wait for it for ages,
But when it comes, it's better than expected.
Something you always remember.
If she were shoes,
She would be my favourite pair of killer heels!
They never get boring and go with every outfit.
She reminds me of Ariel from 'The Little Mermaid',
Fun and easy, but so curious,
In the end, she ends up happy.
As a colour, she would be pink!
It's the colour her cheeks go when she laughs!
If I could wear her, it would definitely be as a T-shirt,
The one of a kind that no one has.
Everyone envies you, because it's yours!
If I saw her in a cake shop,
She would be a French Fancy,
Lovely colour, so petite and almost so pretty,
You don't want to eat it.
She is a Beetle,
If she could be a car,
Cute and small, but an engine that would take you far!

She is my best friend
And if around my neck I could wear her,
She would be my pearl!

Rachel Balmer (13)
Airdrie Academy, Airdrie

Existence

I exist,
I breathe, I see, I hear,
How can we be certain?
We might not even be real.

Feelings don't exist,
They might, but they don't.
A smile can be fake,
The happiness doesn't exist in a fake smile.

Fear exists, pain exists,
No one is really happy.
Nothing makes anyone happy,
Happiness doesn't exist.

My memories don't exist,
I destroyed them long ago.
A pessimist wanting to forget,
Wanting to forget my past existed.

Nothing ever goes right,
The non-existent happiness,
Made me the way I am.
I never had a happiness that really existed,
Not until you appeared in my life.

I am certain a lot of things
Are non-existent.
You messed up everything,
I liked that,
It made me smile,
It wasn't fake.

Emma Lowe (14)
Airdrie Academy, Airdrie

Love Or Loathe

She is sunny - warm and caring, but
She is thunder - loud and scary when things don't go her way.
She is yellow - soft and cheerful, but
She is green - envious and jealous of me.
She is milk - makes you strong when you're weak, but
She is soda water - plain with no taste in clothes.
She is lipgloss - shiny and colourful, but
She is eyeshadow - wrong colour that doesn't suit.
She is strawberries - nice and sweet, but
She is lemons - sour as can be.
She is an action book - full of energy, but
She is a mystery book - doesn't tell you her feelings.
She is a flute - softly played, but
She is a tuba - droning, telling you her worries, but
She is my friend!

Laura Hopton (14)
Airdrie Academy, Airdrie

Lion

A lion is a terrifying predator,
No other animal is better,
Than a lion in the hunt.

He stalks and stalks,
As the tasty prey walks,
Into his deadly trap.

When he thinks the time's right,
He'll use all of his might,
To bring his prey down.

Then, what every animal dreads,
The lion rips them to shreds,
As he wolfs down his meaty feast.

The lion has always been top of the food chain,
On Africa's deadly plain,
Where no creature is safe.

Lex Sharpe (13)
Auchinleck Academy, Auchinleck

A Mother's Grief

One, two,
I took a bullet for you,
Three, four,
The chilling knock at the door,

Five, six,
There are things money can't fix,
Seven, eight,
A mother's heart is filled with hate,

Nine, ten,
I'll never see him again.

Sophie Hall (14)
Aughnacloy College, Aughnacloy

Turn Back Time

How I want to turn back time
Wish I hadn't committed the crime
The CD was on the shelf near the floor
And two minutes later, I was out the door

How I want to turn back time
My guilty conscience on my mind
In my room I'm all alone
And then comes a ring on the phone

How I want to turn back time
Wish I hadn't committed the crime
Life's never been the same
But I'm the only one to blame

How I want to turn back time.

Alison Campbell (14)
Aughnacloy College, Aughnacloy

War's Not The Answer

In silence they pray
For a better today
For a better tomorrow
A day without sorrow.

In darkness they fight
Together all night
They cry and they fall
With no feeling at all.

They shiver and shake
Like a giant earthquake
Their hearts beat like mad;
It rather is sad.

For their families, their fear
Is finally here, as it hurts
And they cry
Many soldiers still die.

One day when they're free
They'll finally see
War's not the answer
As proven by history.

Hannah Crawford (14)
Aughnacloy College, Aughnacloy

Band, Band, Band!

Band, band
Glorious band
I love you
Oh, I do
You're brilliant, you're fab
You're all that I have
You're the one and only band!

Crotchets and quavers
And steady beats
Band caps, blazers
And ties
Bus journeys are always great craic
When Colin gets mad!

Back row babes
Are on the prowl
We never stop, you see
Teenage years
Down the drain
At band, band, band!

Fanfares and flourishes
Marches galore
Lullabies and melodies
Are quite the chore!

Keith gets mad
When we do not practise
Arriving in late
With me and my mates!

Annie, Sarah and Grace too
They're all part of the banding crew
Roughan rock, oh, yes we do
Watch out, we're coming for you!

Joy Coote (14)
Aughnacloy College, Aughnacloy

I Am A Tree

It's hard being me,
I stand all alone,
With leaves falling around me,
Am not able to leave,

It's hard being me,
As I am a tree,
The apples keep falling,
As the wind keeps calling,

Summer is here, I am happy now,
But I am surrounded by cows,
They're eating my leaves and biting my bark
And they will leave me to die, with no heart.

Stewart McAlister (14)
Aughnacloy College, Aughnacloy

All Alone In The Town!

When I was born
I couldn't see
My eyes were closed
As tight as can be.

Just two weeks after
They called me Jasper,
If my tail wiggled,
The children giggled.

But my master opened
The kitchen door,
He stood on my paw
And I yelped, 'Argh! That's sore!'

Now that I'm older
I'm left outside,
No one to talk to
I'm trying to hide.

The reason I'm hiding
Is from my boss
He hit me and kicked me
And I got covered in moss.

Now the children don't giggle
My tail doesn't wiggle
I'm sad and all down
All alone in the town.

Karen Murphy (14)
Aughnacloy College, Aughnacloy

Shopping!

I love to shop and buy lots of things
Lots of clothes and gold diamond rings.

My favourite shops are really great
Like Top Shop, River Island and DV8.

I go out shopping with my mates,
To buy an outfit for my date.

Sometimes I shop with Mum and Dad
But when they see the price, they often go mad.

I love glittery beads and Elizabeth Arden
But Mum keeps yapping, she wants back to the garden.

There's one more shop I have to go to
That's NV for a pair of shoes.

I need slippers, socks and pyjamas
But by this time, my mum is bananas.

I have finally come to the end of my shop
My mum is happy now, she's going home to mop.

Shareen McMaster (14)
Aughnacloy College, Aughnacloy

The Imagination

The imagination is a powerful thing,
For in your mind, you're the king.
The way it works can make you full,
Of happy thoughts or even dull.

Think of all those wonderful things,
Cars and music, what joy they bring.
No matter which mood you are in,
Feeling down or in the bin.

Oh, yes the imagination,
So full of self-creation.

Philip Caddoo (14)
Aughnacloy College, Aughnacloy

My Dog Skip

My dog Skip,
He's nicknamed Pip.
He wanders alone,
While looking for a bone.

He moves so fast,
How long will it last?
He chases the foxes,
From the chicken boxes.

His long, fluffy coat,
Is now turning grey.
He used to be happy,
But now he's just snappy.

My dog Skip,
He's nicknamed Pip.
Has a place in my heart,
So we'll never part.

Gillian Brush (14)
Aughnacloy College, Aughnacloy

All Alone Now

I used to have a family
Where I always did feel loved,
But now it has all changed
From my master above.

I had a lovely basket
And slept inside the house,
But now I'm in the garden
In a little wooden house.

He used to always love it
When I'd wag my tail in glee,
But now that it's all different
He never comes to see.

One day we both got in the car
I finally did feel great,
But now I'm left all alone
In a big, vast, open space.

Sarah Morrow (14)
Aughnacloy College, Aughnacloy

Scottish Premier

S hining Saints up for promotion
C ompetition over with Gretna promoted
O h surprise, surprise, Celtic first, Rangers second
T itle over by Christmas
T wo teams in the Champion's League next season
I nverness Caly not so ballistic this time
S t Mirren four points clear, but for how long?
H umped the hoops at Celtic Park Rangers back in business at last

P ies at Pittodrie, the only good bit at Pittodrie
R angers rolling unbeat since new boss
E dinburgh hearts looking for new boss again
M otherwell losing, McDonald down, next season I would say
I n last position, will Dunfermline escape relegation
E hiogu overhead kick, Rangers win at last
R angers rule, Celtic drool!

Robert McClymont (14)
Banchory Academy, Banchory

Ma Wee Toot

Ma wee cat
Bonnie 'n' cute
Cuddles 'n' luvin
That's ma wee Toot
Jumping aroon the hoose
Catchin' a wee moose
Funny 'n' playful
That's ma wee Toot
Black 'n' white
Mad 'n' happy
That's ma wee Toot

Ma wee Toot
Always jumpin' aboot
Waggin' his tail
Even fin he's chasin' a snail
Every day his gin aboot
Trying to chase a wee moose
Opening the catflap out 'n' in
On till it's time tee be fed
Then he goes to his bed.

Marie Ewen (14)
Banchory Academy, Banchory

Gangster

I am a gangster,
I have lost my parents,
They were killed in a shootout,
All I can feel is hate.

It feels as if I am being swallowed,
By this endless loathing and pain,
I have no future,
All I desire is revenge.

As I walk down the street,
Closed-down shops,
Abandoned flats,
Are all I can see.

My gang are having a fight,
The guys are looking scared,
The enemy gang is coming,
But I am ready for them.

I reach into my hoodie pocket,
I can feel the gun handle,
I pull it out,
I feel a surge of power.

The dark outlines of figures,
Come running out of the mist,
I lift my gun up,
I am ready to kill.

My finger slowly pulls back the trigger,
That will unleash the angel of death,
But I am pulled back by a bullet,
I was too late and I am about to die.

I can feel the hot steel,
Implanted in my chest,
The warm blood contrasts
And is dripping down my body.

Why am I not dead?
I feel uneasy and am struggling to breathe,
I know I am not properly dead,
Because I failed to avenge my parents.

I feel like a failure,
I will never rest in peace,
Life is unfair,
I have known this all my life.

Today, I know this for a fact,
I have learned a valuable lesson,
But I will never live to tell the tale,
For I am gone forever.

Mathew Miller (13)
Bearsden Academy, Bearsden

Through The Eyes Of A Soldier

On the 8th of June, 1917
During the first Great War,
General Brown marched his troops slowly
To the marshy trenches of the south of England.
He had great pity for his men, because
His commanders told him it was a suicide
But they would go to bide time so defences could be constructed.
They put up camp, with scorching fires,
This eased my pain and betrayal.
His army ate stale, maggot-infested bread
And tasteless, cold broth, then went to bed.
On that fatal day
The merciless Germans invaded the border
And then marched towards the trenches
Of General Brown in great numbers.
General Brown stood to a magnificent hill
With great oak trees and little shrubs infested with wildlife.
He stood watching the slaughter,
He had lied and cheated his men.
He could not take it anymore,
General Brown took his horse and rode down the hill
In a frenzy of screaming and shouting.
Later, after the battle
The remaining English soldiers searched the battlefield
For any survivors.
They had won the battle and fought off the savage Germans.
After five minutes, an excited soldier shouted, 'Survivor!'
It was General Brown.

Alexander Hendry (12)
Bearsden Academy, Bearsden

Being A Baby

I wish I were still a baby,
You have all the freedom in the world
And can get away with anything you do wrong.
You get all the attention you want
And your parents do everything for you, around the clock,
But crying is the one thing you cannot stop.
You have to eat what is given to you,
Although most of the time, it comes back up as something else.
People don't stop squeezing you,
Then you stop needing to go to the loo.
Now I realise, being a baby isn't so great,
But being a teenager, is not much of a better fate.

Ranjeev Panesar (13)
Bearsden Academy, Bearsden

War

As the sound of bullets ring in my ear
I hide behind a broken-down plane
In hope this will all stop
But it just gets worse.

I'm sweating with the heat
And shivering with the cold
I feel like crying
Too scared to move.

I am a young woman from Iraq
And my homeland is being invaded
I sit surprisingly still
And I'm too shocked to breathe.

I take one look out of the window
As a man turns round to see
My eyes light up and I breathe once more
The window smashes, a bullet cuts me down
On me, life has shut its door.

Craig Wallace (14)
Bearsden Academy, Bearsden

Homeless

I see people with family and friends,
As I sit there on my own, next to the bin.
People wear designer clothes,
I just have these rags I found.
I see people with money,
Buying things they want, but don't need,
I just sit there with nothing.
People are sitting in cafes eating and drinking,
I have nothing but food from the bin.
Some people are reading books,
I only have the newspaper I stole.
I hear laughter and talk,
As I just lie there all on my own.

Adam MacLeod (12)
Bearsden Academy, Bearsden

My Gran

When she tries to speak, no one hears
Not even her.
When she laughs, it comes out loud and proud
Because that's all she can do.
When she needs someone, no one's there.
When she cries, no sound, just tears.
When she falls, no one sees.
When she looks, she can't understand
And no one cares, only me.

Amy Thomson (13)
Bearsden Academy, Bearsden

The Meaning Of Life

The meaning of life is always good, so it should
The animals, big and small, furry or bald, I don't care
You should cherish the little things, like the green, green grass
The countryside with the big hairy cows
The forest with trees and all living things
These are not little things, they're big, big things, but nobody cares
I do, I care about the animals
I care about the countryside
The forest too
I cherish everything, the sun, the houses
The people that keep the world going
I have a reason to get up in the morning and so do you
The sun to have fun
If it rains, I'll still have fun
I work hard and always try, I never give up
That's the meaning of life to me, to you.

Stephen Dickie (12)
Bearsden Academy, Bearsden

Seeing Through One Another's Eyes

It is as hot as a burning furnace,
The sun beats down on the broken land,
The cracks run through the ground,
Which was once soil,
There are no crops or flowers to be found,
Anywhere.

I long to eat,
Just one decent meal,
All we have is straggly wheat,
But then we sell it,
To make ends meet,
Just the same old crops.

We have no running water,
Or proper toilets or baths,
I have to travel many miles every day,
Collect water and carry it home,
I do this every single day,
All for a drink.

I own two items of clothing,
A home-made T-shirt
And trousers that fray,
They are not great, but they are clothes,
Did I mention that I wear my clothes every day,
All the time?

But one thing I know,
I am like you, normal,
We both play, all day if we could,
I don't eat a lot of food,
Like you do,
But we are equal, the same.

Rebekah Hemming (13)
Bearsden Academy, Bearsden

Another Person's Eyes

I am a young boy, four coming on five,
Why don't you take a look through my eyes?
It is the middle of summer,
But I don't get to play,
Instead I get up and work all day.

It's as hot as an oven,
But I don't get to stop,
I look out of my house
And see all my friends play,
How I wish I would be like them some day.

I get up every morning,
Just at the break of dawn,
I walk two miles to get clean water,
If I don't, then we have to use the old river,
It's not exactly clean.

I work for my sister and mother,
To take the place of my big brother,
He too worked hard,
I feel bad about what he did, I took him for granted,
I'm truly sorry for that,
Now I'll never get to thank him.

I feel quite terrible,
It's the end of my days,
I'm just wondering,
Who will take my place?

Dayle Hassan (13)
Bearsden Academy, Bearsden

Silent Speaker

I am the silent speaker
All alone in the dark
Lonely, abandoned, sad.
I am the silent speaker
I wish for a home with
Love, happiness and fun.
I am the silent speaker
I want my scream to be heard
Louder than all those who speak
Noisy, loud, clear.
I am the silent speaker
Never to speak
Never to be heard
My voice is building up inside of me
Wanting out
But just bouncing around inside of me
Unable to escape.
I am the silent speaker
My life feels over
I want to escape
But I can't and I fade away
Day by day.

Caitlin Ord (12)
Bearsden Academy, Bearsden

What It Would Be Like If You Couldn't Speak

People take speaking for granted,
They shout, scream and talk too much.
Imagine what it would be like if you couldn't speak,
People could talk to you,
Then shout if you didn't reply.
You could never get your point across,
You wouldn't be able to tell your best friend a secret.
All of your feelings, trapped inside,
With no way to let them out.
You would be scared of what could happen next,
All alone,
In your quiet, little world.
Think of all the things,
You wouldn't be able to do . . .
Like say *I do* at your wedding,
Tell your children how much you love them,
You wouldn't be able to make new friends,
Or get a job because . . .
You can't say anything at the interview.
All your time spent worrying
Where you would have gone or will go in life.
All dreadful things to have to go through,
But there would be one thing that would
Help you through all of that . . .
Your family.

Caitlin Doyle (12)
Bearsden Academy, Bearsden

The Tree

Why do you cut me down?
I am important for I help you live.
Why do you cut me down?
I have feelings just as you have as well.
Why do you cut me down?
I give you inspiration for paintings.
Why do you cut me down?
I do not understand why you do this to me.
Why do you cut me down?
I have just as many rights as you do.
Why do you cut me down?
I have stood for hundreds of years, but still.
Why do you cut me down?
I don't deserve to be treated this way.
Why do you cut me down?
I haven't done anything wrong, so why?
Why do you cut me down?
I amaze people from all around the world.
Why do you cut me down?
I am being destroyed by nature as well.
Why do you cut me down?
I watch in horror as you cut us down,
So please plant me, water me, care for me and love me,
Please, don't cut me down.

Louise McCormick (12)
Bearsden Academy, Bearsden

Good Times, Great Memories

Dodgems screeching and crashing
Frights on the biggest roller coaster
Candyfloss floating round and round

Coconuts cracking against the ground
People towering on stilts
Clowns intimidating me with jokes

Teddy bears sitting miserably on the stall
Hammers hitting people
Goldfish swimming round their bags

Horses bobbing on the roundabout
Stripy circus tent standing tall
Little children standing small

I watch my colourless world.

Fiona Byrne (12)
Bearsden Academy, Bearsden

Good Times . . . Great Memories

The day I learnt to ride my bike . . .
I was so proud of myself.
The day I learnt to swim . . .
I spent so much time practising.
All the times I've laughed . . .
With friends and family.
All the times I've cried . . .
At sad things and when people have died.
Playing in puddles . . .
Because there was nothing to do in the house.
Or lying in the sun . . .
Wishing the sun would never go away.
Or when I lost my dog . . .
I spent days looking for it.
Some good . . . some bad . . .
But best of all . . .
Climbing the trees at Castle Toward
That was so exciting
The day it rained from day to night
There was absolutely nothing to do!
The one Christmas it snowed . . .
It was up to my knees!
The time my wee cousin was born . . .
I felt much bigger and happy
So many memories . . .
Some miserable, some glad . . .
All my memories, good and bad.

Anna Higgins (12)
Bearsden Academy, Bearsden

Broken Friendship

Harsh words spoken
No meaning
Lashing out
No control
Hurt and anger
Empty heart
Pleading for forgiveness
But not out loud
Needing help
But coping on your own
Permanent scars
Internally
Now silence echoes between us
No words escape our lips
Sitting alone
I decide I have to correct what happened
I have to make things right
No matter what I do.

Caitlin Chalmers (13)
Bearsden Academy, Bearsden

Dog's Hope

My old owner, I hated her
She hurt me
I remember that day
She abandoned me
No food
No drink
I was left all alone
In a dark alley
No warmth
No love
No hope.
Then, that day it came, hope
A glowing light at the end of the alley
A family to care for me
They took me to their warm home
They fed me
They loved me
And I loved them
They restored my hope.

Holly Shearer (12)
Bearsden Academy, Bearsden

I Am A Fox

I am a soft breeze, sweeping through the streets
I am under the twinkling stars, guiding me
My ears are pricked, I'm silently aware
Under the bright lights, with their glinting glare
Slick and sly is the human's stereotype
Yet, I'm startled and vulnerable in the night
I sprint across the busy avenue
They yowl at me, the area is new
I'm lost and lonely, in the rain
I dash back down the old dirt lane
I curl up in my fur, so fluffy and red
My green eyes sparkling, in my small, clever head
Can you guess which animal I am?
I am the fox, minute and calm.

Jade Ellen Sturrock (12)
Bearsden Academy, Bearsden

Looking At The World In Someone Else's Eyes

Cribs look like jails to me,
big bars not letting me go free.
With animals printed on my covers,
saying 'roar' and 'hiss'.

Mum and Dad came in my room,
stroking my head and kissing my forehead.
They turn off the light and leave me,
I'm not hungry, I'm not sad, I'm just scared of the dark.

The end of the crib Floppy Ears is sitting,
with his big long ears and white furry belly.
He may be a teddy but he is my friend
and I want him to come and play.

When the sun outside is blazing,
Mum comes up and takes me.
She gives me a bottle from the table.
After a while she rubs my back
and all of a sudden a roar pops out.

My dad plays toys with me,
with floppy ears, Spider-Man and Tigger.
He does these voices but they don't
speak like that in my mind.

Whenever I say a word,
Mum and Dad go crazy,
they say I'm a good boy
and want me to say it again.

At night Dad and Mum
sing me a lullaby
and I fall asleep
for the night to go by.

Sophie Wayt (13)
Bearsden Academy, Bearsden

What Do You See?

Look at the world through someone else's eyes
What do you see?
Do you see happiness? Sadness?
All I see is change
Change for the better, change for the worse
Whether we are fighting a war we cannot win
Or polluting our air with unneeded fumes
Or destroying habitats of wild animals
Forcing them to extinction
Wiping them off our Earth like an unneeded stain
Their home just like ours gone
Precious land that we know so well
So beautiful, so fine, destroyed
Used as land to build on
The unfair treatment of people still goes on
It's here! It's there! It's everywhere!
Don't we all have equal rights?
Then why are we treated with such disrespect
A world we were once proud of
Look at it now, what would you say?
Litter piling up on the street
Some people too scared to leave their homes
Crime and gangs all around
When I look at the world I'm not proud
To see what my generation has done
After dark I feel scared to go out
Like many others I feel intimidated by others
Look at the world
Look very hard
What do you see?

Holly Munn (14)
Bearsden Academy, Bearsden

I Want To Be Remembered . . .

I want to be remembered,
For the rest of time,
I want future generations to wonder,
What went through my mind,
They will probably think I was crazy,
But I actually am quite sane.

I want to be remembered,
For the rest of time,
Isn't that what everyone wants,
Deep within their minds?

You may think I'm evil,
Maybe I really am,
But now I will be remembered,
For the rest of time.

Rhonda Stewart (12)
Bellshill Academy, Bellshill

I Can't Help That I'm Blind!

I can't help that I'm blind,
It's not my fault I was born like this!

Red, yellow, green and blue,
No colour matters to me,
Because I can't see them, can I?
It's nothing but blackness in my lonely world.

Never will I see the face of a newborn baby,
Nor the faces of the people whom I call family.
Day and night have always been the same,
The sun, moon, stars and clouds will always remain a mystery,
I can only imagine what they look like
And I'll never know.

How do you think you would feel in my world?
Names thrown at you at every opportunity,
I can't help being this way!

Just because I can't see, doesn't mean I'm stupid,
I do have feelings too, you know!
I'm just another person,
Just remember,
I can't help being blind!

Nikki Tobin (12)
Bellshill Academy, Bellshill

Teacher From Hell

Part One
'First Year! I am not speaking over you!'
The voice of the Devil speaks once again!
Will he ever stop shouting from the depths of Hell?
With his roars, he shakes the ground around.

He lifts his knee upon a chair
And gives you the scary glare.
With his half-moon specs and baldy head,
He roars, 'First Years! This is getting out of hand!'

Part Two
Look at those little twits from Hell,
With their high-risen collars and 'cool' hair gel.
They make me seem like a stupid clown,
Shouting all day and making me frown.

These little freaks are all the same,
Driving me mad all over again.
But when Friday comes and the bell rings loud,
I'm out first - ahead of the crowd!

Jack Paton, Edwin Lau (12) & Callum Bulloch (13)
Bellshill Academy, Bellshill

The Soldier

Many times I've gone to war,
Didn't know what we were fighting for.

Away to fight in a distant land,
Marching across its golden sand.

Lots of lives have been lost,
At a very bloody cost.

Death is what we're destined to,
But it all depends on what we do.

The war goes on for many days,
Victory's like defeat in many ways.

War is sometimes very cruel,
On the basis of conquer and rule.

Fighting for our lives and pride,
Though it's the same on the enemy's side.

But it doesn't matter what side your own,
Because we are simply just Death's pawn.

Richard Lovell & Joshua Abraham (12)
Bellshill Academy, Bellshill

The Final Conversion

The stadium was at a standstill;
All eyes on me.
If I miss, will I be dropped?
What am I thinking?
Be positive.

It's a simple kick:
Training ground stuff.
It will be easy,
No problem at all.
My coach knows I can do it,
I can see it on his face.

We have had a bad season,
Although we have come so far.
I want to be well-known,
For my almighty kicking,
Superb power
And my great team spirit.

I step up: this is my chance.
All concentration on the ball,
The tension is the stadium is building,
The crowd silences.
Concentrating completely,
I strike the ball,
I connect perfectly,
I know it's won us the match!

Marc Rodgers & Robbie McCrone (13)
Bellshill Academy, Bellshill

Baxter, My Cuddly Toy

I wake up hearing gunshots,
Bombing and disaster,
I hear my mum scream, 'Argh!'
Then I reach for Baxter,
My cuddly toy.

I try to get to sleep,
But I feel things won't change,
Sitting in the darkness,
Gives me the creeps again,
Then I reach for Baxter,
My cuddly toy.

At last, it's stopped,
Sirens and all,
No more Mummy screaming,
No more rattling walls,
Then I hug Baxter,
My cuddly toy.

Everything stays silent,
For a little while,
Then it starts once again,
Even more vile,
Then I grab for Baxter,
But Baxter is gone . . .

Debi Gardiner (12)
Bellshill Academy, Bellshill

My Room

Wind blowing through the window,
Curtains rustle and flap,
Grass pollen blowing through the vent,
Mingles with the scent of cooking from downstairs.

A brown furry bear,
Looks down from the top of a dusty wardrobe,
Smiles towards his long-time friend,
Rocky Racoon.

At night, kind of creepy,
Faces lighting up in the moonlight,
Always giving me nightmares,
Never slept a wink.

So many things in one small room,
Seem harmless in daytime,
But at night . . .

Caroline Hassan (14)
Bellshill Academy, Bellshill

The Lottery Winner

I can't believe I've got the lot!
Every number, I've hit the jackpot!
I never thought I'd actually win,
I can see the money pouring in.

My life will never be the same,
All of this from just a game,
I wonder how I'll spend the dosh,
It could be on something very posh.

Perhaps a yacht or even a plane,
Or a Ferrari to drive my wallet insane,
Maybe I'll live in sunny Spain,
Where they hardly see the rain.

A chef to cook me fine cuisine,
The biggest mansion you've ever seen,
Of course, I'll need to find my ticket
And hope that no one has tried to nick it!

Elliot Shepka (12)
Bellshill Academy, Bellshill

How Long Will It Be?

How long will it be until I'm on flat land?
How long will be it until people fully understand?
How long will it be until people don't see me as an outcast?
How long will it be until I can forget the past?
How long will it be until people see as I do?
How long will it be until I feel like one of you?
How long will it be until I meet someone I can trust?
How long will it be until I don't feel so fussed?
I want you to all see,
That I can be free,
If you give me a chance and accept me.

Gemma McLean & Rachel Stewart (13)
Bellshill Academy, Bellshill

It's Only Just A . . .

It's only just a letter
Why'd you want it? I'm much better

It's only just a plant
Even if it was from an aunt

It's only just a shoe
Even if it were brand, spanking new

It's only just a fluffy bunny
What? Am I the only one who thinks it's funny?

It's only just a little rat
So why'd you hit it with a baseball bat?

It's only just a tiled floor
Now it matches that brown door

And after all I've done
I've been left with no one
Now I'm alone by myself
In a bare house, with a broken shelf
I think I'll die in this house
Now I'll lie down and be as quiet as a mouse.

Andrew Baxter (12)
Bellshill Academy, Bellshill

Life On The Street

I stand in the cold, watching people go past,
I wait for a person to give me some cash.

Others give me a really bad name,
For buying drugs like heroin and cocaine.

Hunger and thirst are familiar feelings,
Because of the men with the dirty dealings.

To a normal life, I could never go back,
As a result of the things I lack.

Love and trust are things of the past,
Somehow I knew they would never last.

I have no ambition; no job, no pay,
I have no direction; I've lost my way.

Kelsey Caldwell & Nadia Murphy (12)
Bellshill Academy, Bellshill

Last Hour To Live

As blood drips from the knife,
Tears drips from my face.
As blood flows from my wrists,
Tears flow from my eyes.

As pain cuts through me,
Misery cuts through me.
As the pain becomes worse,
The misery becomes worse.

As a physical wound is re-opened,
A bad memory is re-visited.
As the physical wounds become visible,
The bad memories become visible.

As life seeps from me,
Blood drips from me,
Tears flow from me,
Pain cuts through me,
The misery becomes greater
And then it stops
And the world is gone.

Cara Jane Kingsley (13)
Boclair Academy, Bearsden

Heaven

I wonder what Heaven looks like
I'm sure it's really bright!
What with all those angels
Shining in the light!

I wonder what Heaven sounds like
I'm sure it's really loud!
What with all those angels
Dancing on the clouds!

I wonder what Heaven smells like
I'm sure it's really sweet!
What with all those flowers
That grow to 30 feet!

I wonder where Heaven is
I'm sure it's not too far!
Just up above the fluffy clouds
And beyond the shining star!

Amy Rooney (13)
Cathkin High School, Cambuslang

Dolphin

Sleek, powerful and playful dolphin,
Dives and tumbles into the ocean.
She looks at the fish,
With a great big grin.
She splashes and somersaults,
She waves her fins and her tail
And gracefully swims away.

Stephanie Morrison (12)
Cathkin High School, Cambuslang

Dad's Taxi

I have my own personal taxi
With my own personal driver
And when I need a lift
I dial a number.

He'll jump in his car
And come straight away
And this happens
Nearly every day.

My driver lives with me
And his name is Dad
And I give him a cuddle
Whenever he's sad.

Nicole Mulrooney (12)
Cathkin High School, Cambuslang

The Dolphin

The dolphin gracefully dives into the ocean
He tumbles powerfully and splashes
The waves start to streamline
He playfully swims
He gets out, then somersaults in once again
Using his fins and tail sleekly.

Chloe Wellington (12)
Cathkin High School, Cambuslang

The Wolf

The sleek wolf runs swiftly
Through the night
Howls and growls
And sniffs its prey
The silver moon
Shines on its coat
And his menacing fangs
Get ready for prey.

Lauren Newbigging (12)
Cathkin High School, Cambuslang

Flowers Are Like People

Flowers are like people,
They're just like you and me.

You may be a rose,
Or even a lily.

Celebs are exotic plants,
That every weed wants to be.

Or you could be a common flower,
For everyone to see.

Maybe you're a sunflower,
To make the world bright.

You could be a winter flower
And come out with the snowy showers.

Flowers are like people,
They are just like you and me.

So think of all the flowers,
Which one would you be?

Lauren Campbell (12)
Cathkin High School, Cambuslang

My Snake Poem

The rough snake coiled up
Hisses as he prepares to strike
And raises his head
Flicking his forked tongue
As he slithers along the ground
Like a rope with scales.

Andrew Law (13)
Cathkin High School, Cambuslang

The Wolf

Has a sleek silver coat
He runs swiftly in the moonlight
He sniffs for his prey in the dead of night
He howls and growls
It's the wolf.

Dale Gray-Gardner (13)
Cathkin High School, Cambuslang

The Dolphin

The dolphin dives into the waves with its fins and it
Tumbles into the waves so powerfully and
It splashes with its tail so sleek
Playfully in the ocean.

Beth Cochrane (12)
Cathkin High School, Cambuslang

The Dolphin

The sleek dolphin
Splashes gracefully as it swims
Somersaults into the waves
With a dive
Playfully tumbles into the ocean
Powerfully.

Sharie Boyd (13)
Cathkin High School, Cambuslang

The Killer Wolf

Sleek moon on a silver night
The wolf comes out menacing about
With his dangerous fangs and his grey spiky coat
He gives a great growl
The dangerous wolf he sniffs upon the air
He holds his head high and howls for his prey
Someone will die . . .

Stephen Ponsonby (13)
Cathkin High School, Cambuslang

World Wrestling Entertainment Mania!
(By a manic fan!)

I adore the WWE -
Because it is so great!
I even think they're my mates -
Batista, Undertaker and
John Cena too!
Plus Torie Wilson, Candice
And Michelle McCool.
I talk to them on the TV -
Although they can't hear me!
And I follow them around:
From America to Jamaica,
From Austria to Bosnia.
I have devoted my whole life -
To following them and finding out
Everything about them . . .
But they know nothing about *me!*

Ross Innes (15)
Cedarbank School, Livingston

The Day I Stood Up To The Bullies

Their nicknames are Bozo and Beater -
They live up to their names!
At first, they ignored me;
Then they started playing games.
They got physical:
They pushed me around;
They punched me;
They kicked me;
They just wanted my pound.
I told the teacher;
They got in trouble;
They shook and they shivered
And they started to bubble.
I was very happy
That they got detention.
As a result
They pay me no attention!

Harley Goldie (15)
Cedarbank School, Livingston

I Remember

I remember when I was young,
I used to have so much fun.
There are good memories and bad,
I remember the worst I had
And it was extremely bad.
I have never felt so alive,
When an entire beehive chased me.

I was in the woods one day
And I was having a bit of a crack.
When suddenly, I felt something
On the back of my neck.
I ran to grab some ice,
Though I only got stung twice.
It was the worst pain in my neck
Now I will always look back.

James McQuade (14)
Christian Brothers Secondary School, Belfast

Why?

Why does the sun shine?
Why are some people blind?
Why does it rain?
Why do we feel pain?

Why do we fight?
Why is there a day and night?
Why do we have to die?
Why do we lie?

Why is snow white?
Why do dogs bite?
Why is a week seven days?
Why do people have funny ways?

Why is the sky blue?
Why are animals kept in a zoo?
Why are mountains high?
Why do we have to say goodbye?

Michael Monaghan (14)
Christian Brothers Secondary School, Belfast

The Youth Of Today - Have Your Say!

I think it's unfair
That we get blamed because we're there!
I think it's not right
That Catholics and Protestants fight!
We shouldn't get the blame
We're not all the same!
I hate when you get moved on
We're not in the wrong!
No matter where we go
Someone complains and puts on a show!
We all get stereotyped
OAPs need not be frightened!
We're not here to cause any trouble
If it were up to some, we would be buried in rubble!
You are young too
Leave us alone, we won't bother you!

Corey Hamill (14)
Christian Brothers Secondary School, Belfast

Good Times, Great Memories

What a great time I had on that day,
Laughing, joking and beginning to play.

All of the family being together,
No problems at all, just great sunny weather.

The end of the night finally kicks in
And all the beers go into the bin.

The uncle's outside, lying there drunk,
He has to go home, there's always the trunk.

We all go home with great big smiles,
While all the drunk relatives slip on the tiles.

But if I remember one thing from this night,
There can be happiness from day until night.

Tony McNeilly (14)
Christian Brothers Secondary School, Belfast

Why?

Why do we die
And not live forever?
Why do we die so young?
Why are there diseases?
Why do people get the urge to kill?
Why are people so stuck up about life?
Why are people criticised for being different?

Why do people get abused?
Why is there no peace in the world?
Why can animals not talk like humans?
Why do people get sick?
Why is there sound?
Why can some people not say what they feel?

Why is the world round?
Why is the sky blue and not purple?
Why do people need to sleep?
Why are school kids so badly behaved?
Why is there no hope?
God only knows why!

Jonathan Copeland (14)
Christian Brothers Secondary School, Belfast

Why?

Why is there racism?
Why is there love?
Why is there sectarianism?
We're supposed to follow the Holy Spirit
Represented by a dove.

Why are we born?
Why do we live?
Lives ripped apart,
Everything . . . so torn.

Why are we thin?
Why are we fat?
Why are we criticised?
Seen as everything we're not?

Why do we live?
Why do we die?
How do we live
Through such chaos and lies?

Why? Oh why? Oh why?
I wish I knew!

Seamus O'Doherty (14)
Christian Brothers Secondary School, Belfast

Good Times - Great Memories

When I look out of my window
And gaze at the stars,
Every time they twinkle,
Always brings me back . . .

It was a Sunday morning
And I was just past Dublin.
'It won't be long,' I said,
'Until I get to Wexford!'

Three days had passed
And things had changed, endlessly,
From good to bad and bad to good,
I don't think it will stop.

Two days remain now,
I had a go at golf,
My friend missed his mark
And nearly knocked me out!

The final day arrived
And I said goodbye to all the new friends I found
And began to travel,
Back to my home,
Far away from them.

So, every time I gaze at the stars,
I am always reminded of Wexford
And there is hope in my heart,
To return there one more time
And meet the friends I found, again.

Mark Murtagh (16)
Christian Brothers Secondary School, Belfast

Why Am I Here?

At the dawn of time,
Was there a god?
Was the universe big?
Was there a bang?

Our past -
Do we have a task?
If we are born,
Why do we die?

Before the bang,
Was there a past? Ancient empires?
Perhaps this god thought it would be fun -
Fun to show the world how to run.

Fear enters our souls,
Then why are we so cold?
Maybe it's only our nature -
The nature of human imperfection.

Patrick McCorry (16)
Christian Brothers Secondary School, Belfast

Turn Back Time

If I could turn back time,
I would make all food nice.
If I could turn back time,
I would go on holiday again.
If I could turn back time,
I would go back in time to my birthday.
If I could turn back time,
I would change everything that I have done wrong and make it right again.
If I could turn back time,
I would go to the Man Utd match that I went to before.
If I could turn back time,
I would keep going back and forward so that I don't get older.
If I could turn back time,
I would try and save everyone who injured themselves or died.
If I could turn back time,
I would go back in time when there was a war and see what it was like.
If I could turn back time,
I would go back in time and tell everyone what was going to happen.
If I could turn back time,
I would go back in time and find out the lottery numbers
and then I would tell someone in my family.
Then they would win.
If I could turn back time,
I would find out everything about Jesus
and tell everyone the truth in later life.
If I could turn back time,
I would try and do different things that I have never done before.

Stephen Wylie (15)
Christian Brothers Secondary School, Belfast

Guardian Of The Birds

He sits there on the grassy hillside,
As he smiles into the gentle breeze blowing upon his face
And looks up at the sunset-filled sky,
The birds dance around the colourful clouds,
On their wings of silver and gold,
Singing softly to their master.

The night sky arrives, the moon is at its full,
He's still sitting on the hill, watching the moonlight,
Shimmer onto the glistening river.
His wings are of angelic white,
He smiles at his little friends
And shuffles his wings gently,
His loose feathers dance in the wind.

The master of the moon and sky,
Guardian of the birds.
He smiles and watches his friends,
Dancing in the air without a care,
Welcoming him to the sky,
So he lifts his wings gracefully and flies up to greet them.

He smiles at them one last time,
Bidding them farewell and disappears,
His silver feathers fall to the ground;
The moonlight shines on them.
Farewell guardian of the birds!
And all the birds with their wings of silver and gold,
Fly off into the moonlit night.

Amy Robinson (13)
Drumglass High School, Dungannon

Haunted House

The house at the bottom of my street is haunted,
By a man who was tormented and taunted.
As his wife's blood ran down the walls,
He ran screaming down the halls, 'Help! Murder!' he cried,
But his wife had already died.
On Hallowe'en my friend and I stepped into that house,
The door slammed shut and darkness swept in . . .
The only sound was a mouse.
I flicked on the torch and witnessed a sight,
That would allow me no sleep for many a night.
Dust and decay, but a figure was clear,
It was a man, who saw our faces, portraying fear.
'Don't be scared,' he said in a low voice,
'It wasn't you who killed my beloved Joyce.'
'No Sir, not I,' I said with denial.
'I want to show you something,' he said with a smile.
We obeyed his command
And took hold of his hand,
As he led us through his once wonderful palace.
Little did we know, that within his mind,
He harboured us thoughts of malice.
'Go into that room,' he said with a growl
'And you will see a sight so gruesome and foul.'
We opened the door
And gazed at the floor,
Where lay a withered old woman
And all of the while, behind us with a smile,
The tormented man stood looming.
He bid us farewell and said, 'You kids are too clever.'
When he shut the door with a loud boom . . . *forever!*

Chimene Samson (13)
Forfar Academy, Forfar

Tom (7)

I wish that no one got sick
And the clocks of death did not tick.
I wish everyone had money
And could fill their aching tummies.
I wish that no one got sad
And were always content and glad.

Could all the wishing in the world,
Make these dreams come true?
I wish I understood,
After all I'm only seven.

Every three seconds a child must die poverty-stricken.
How is this? Why?
A dancer's dream dashed when paralysed.
He can't see anything; he has fear in his eyes.
A beautiful girl is down and depressed,
Why can't she see, with beauty she's blessed?

Why must these things happen,
Or is it not my place to say?
In God I must trust,
But is He even here?

Becca Fletcher (14)
Forfar Academy, Forfar

A Writer's Block

I put pen to paper
And I know I can write.
About life, about death,
About day, about night.

But then I stop,
The words will not flow.
I feel like the world,
Is beginning to slow.

I look round the room,
For ideas I might find.
But nothing comes up,
There's a block in my mind.

Nothing gets in,
Nothing gets out.
Voices in my head,
Are beginning to shout.

Make them stop!
Make them go away!
But each one's adamant,
They're going to stay.

Why do they scream?
Why do they squeal?
Why do I care?
I know they're not real!

I'll try listening to them,
It is worth a try.
The voices I hear,
I'm sure wouldn't lie.

I look, I read and then,
I can write again.

Eilidh McMinn (14)
Forfar Academy, Forfar

Imagine

Imagine . . .
You can see yourself on a peak of a mountain
Or flying over the moon,
On top of the Empire State Building
Climbing a tree.

Imagine . . .
You can see yourself on an underground train
Or burning in a volcano,
Deep in the bottom of the sea
Buried in a hole.

Dreaming on a mountain
Wishing on the moon
Smiling on a roof
Singing in a tree.

Worrying on a train
Screaming in a volcano
Downhearted in the sea
Scared in a hole

. . . Idealism or realism?

Rachel Findlay (14)
Forfar Academy, Forfar

Perfect

You see the way I look at you
I see the way you look at me
And all the thoughts of us, I see
No one would believe

I wanna be perfect
Just like you
I wanna be perfect
To love you.

I wish that love could set us free
As together, we live in harmony.
No one tells us right or wrong
For what we have, our love is strong.

Two lives apart, two secrets kept
Our feelings we don't know.
We keep them hush, we keep them near
It's our little secret.

I wanna be perfect
Just like you
I wanna be perfect
To love you.

I sent you my love
From the brightest little star.
Lonely and full of hurt
As the time comes, we will meet.

At school we know
Our love could never be.
As life will be full of laughter
I turn to music to think of you.

I wanna be perfect
When the time comes
I wanna be perfect
Just for you.

Christina Ilia (14)
Forfar Academy, Forfar

RAF Pilot

On the runway
Waiting to take off
I think of the Luftwaffe
And how they scoffed.
Ghosts of the past
Flying aloft
Disappear in the wake
Of the Tornado GR4.
Past meets present
Present meets past
With a resilience
And commitment
Made to last.
This is the right stuff
British and true
And we salute you
The red, white and blue.

Robert Jardine (14)
Glencryan School (SEN), Cumbernauld

Car

My car
Is red and shining
And moves as fast
As lightning
Along a dark and
Gloomy street.
As I listen to the beat
And push the pedals
With my feet
I think that
This is neat.

As I picked up the pace
Along the A805
I realised then
I was finally
Alive.

As a boy racer
I chased my pals
Along the A805
Until the lights
Pierced my eyes
Then a bang
Blackness
And
Failure to survive.

Robert David Morrison Wright (13)
Glencryan School (SEN), Cumbernauld

In The Hospital

I could see the
Modern building
In the distance -
Yorkhill Hospital -
I didn't know
What to expect
But I wanted to go in
And have the hernia
Healed.

My mum was with me
And my PSP too.
The reception
Was crowded
But people looked
Happy.
The nurses put me
In a bed
And then I was taken
To the operating
Theatre.

I was in there at 3.45pm
And out at 5.45pm.
The hernia was gone.
I had stitches
And they were sore.
I was off for a week
Then I went back to school
On Wednesday.

William Walker (14)
Glencryan School (SEN), Cumbernauld

Dirt Bikes

I was only
Twelve years old
When I got into
Dirt bikes.
I asked for one
But my dad said
They were
Too dangerous.

My mum said
I could get one
So I went to
Mickey Oats
And got a
KX85.
I went out on it
Very fast
So my dad said
'So you want to go
To Harkhill to race
On Saturday?'
So, I said, 'Yes.'

I got my suit
For the dirt bike -
Total cost £185 -
And one of
The best days
Of my life.
Priceless.

Scott Forsyth (13)
Glencryan School (SEN), Cumbernauld

Rain

Raindrops are tears
They brush their lips to my skin
In contemplation

Raindrops are fears
Pulling their icy talons through my hair
In sheer interrogation

Raindrops enclose memories
Maybe the kind people wish to forget

Raindrops fall down lovingly
With no time to forgive or regret

A fear of the vain
Is something unmissed
But to dance in the rain
Is to wallow in bliss.

Heather Sinclair (13)
Hamilton Grammar School, Hamilton

Lost In The Woods

I stand here all alone
I stand here late at night
I hear owls hooting
And the tree branches swaying.
I am lost and I don't know what to do
I am really scared, the wolves are barking
I may not return home
And I will never see light again
I'll stay here alone
Forever.

Kelly Macnaught (13)
Hamilton Grammar School, Hamilton

By The Tree

He said he would meet me,
Over there by the tree,
There is nothing but darkness,
Darkness and me.

All I can do,
Is wait right here,
Silent and alone,
Overwhelmed by my fear.

Oh no; I hear movement,
I thought, *I'm going to die,*
Then he appeared,
I let out a sigh.

We walked off together,
Hand in hand,
The trees are still there,
In that dark, lonely land.

Eilidh Laird (13)
Hamilton Grammar School, Hamilton

Tiger By Twilight

The sky is dark,
The moon is bright,
The breeze sweeps softly by.
A noise is heard,
A frightful noise,
A startling, piercing cry.

The trees are gnarled,
The water is clear,
A reflection can just be seen.
A face, an animal,
A tiger is there,
Her large eyes sparkling green.

The coat, the tail,
The large clawed paws,
The beauty of this creature.
But the eyes,
The sparkling bright green eyes,
Are the most outstanding feature.

Her back is arched,
Her paws are spread,
Is heard, a baited breath.
Her eyes gleam brightly,
As she thinks ahead,
A creature must face its death.

She pounces, then roars,
Then stands up proud,
Her green eyes sparkling so bright.
This tiger,
This beautiful tiger,
Creeps quietly off into the night . . .

Vanessa McEwan (13)
Hamilton Grammar School, Hamilton

The Night

Vast chasm of darkness,
Running through the night,
Nothing for miles around,
Just nothingness and the night,
No stars or moon,
Or owls or bats,
I stand here alone,
Just me and the night.

The darkness surrounds me,
A presence I sense,
Not loving or caring,
Just dark and despairing,
As the night grows,
The oxygen vanishes,
I die here alone,
Just me and the night.

Ross Malley
Hamilton Grammar School, Hamilton

Double Standard

Deaden my heart, tell it I am numb.
I will not feel, for what I feel is weak.
Tears, they are not falling from my eyes -
I will not care. I turn the other cheek.

Inside - fire to burn, consume, erupt;
Chip at this dam, no crack or fissure shows.
Inside, I feel so much more than I divulge -
A mass of feelings, but anger overflows.

But I, within myself, am not so strong.
You can cry - I will think no less of you,
But I can never seem to let my feelings go -
I long to tell the truth, as others do.

Cáragh Cassidy (13)
Harberton School, Belfast

The Thriving Mausoleum

Obnoxious fumes filled the room with a solitary approach
Curling with elegance around vases and the clasp of the brooch
Aria stood in an incurable trance, blood falling from the abrasion
Eyes fixed on the nightmare of repulsion known as a social occasion
Disgust scarred her face, as the metallic embrace fell away
from the graze
As she watched the Master reward his hound with heartfelt praise.

The clock flashed three hundred houses and still Atia lay awake
Tossing and turning as she feverishly awaited dawn's break
The recurring nightmare wouldn't cease even in the earliest hours
As she continued to replay the dreaded blood showers
The cracking hum of the trigger came louder with each rewind
And the cackling laughter of the Master was causing her
to lose her mind.

Dawn broke the skies harshly with the early birds' cries
As the venom sinks further into the victims' blind eyes
Collapsing at the sundial with little strength left
She scrawls the story in stone, of her life's undeserved theft
For all the mistreatment and the injections, those humane or obscene
She finally falls unconscious and her death is unseen.

The rumble of the engine screamed insanity as on drove the hearse
Followed by a league of those too suffering from the Master's curse
The priest muttered with disgust when he saw the infested flock
With a glance of terror, he tossed the coffin overboard
and bolts the lock
The lid came up at once and from within arose a black bouquet
Driving on; Aria led the army of the living dead
Wishing to cause naught but havoc and dismay.

Kristina Hopps (15)
Hermitage Academy, Helensburgh

A Lovely Day

Fat pigeons losing their fluff
Like a moulting dog
But yet your feet are a mouldy green colour
Like a frog.

The sun is gleaming like a massive ball of cheese
After the winter we had, it's sure to please
Daffodils poking out the ground
Like lions pouncing on their prey.

Silver rubbish glinting in the sunlight
Like mirrors on a pond
The sparrows dancing on the grass
The music is the wind
What a lovely day!

Pamela Ross (12)
Hermitage Academy, Helensburgh

The Sun

Like a great ball of light it brightens the sky
A never-ending light that's fiery and bright.

Just hanging in the sky with nothing to do except shine
Playing with the fluffy marshmallows and watching the planes go by.

When a storm is approaching it hides behind the clouds
And when the storm disappears it comes back out again
                                              and shouts, *'Boo!'*

Aimee MacPhail (12)
Hermitage Academy, Helensburgh

You Shine In My Life

You remind me of a flower glowing in the sky
You remind me of celery sitting peacefully in the ground
You creep and crawl but don't speak at all
You're as tall as the sky and you're green in the light
You are white as snow and sometimes low
You are blue as my shirt
You are clear as ice and at night you are my delight
You shoot through the sky like birds going by.

Mollie Sheard (12)
Hermitage Academy, Helensburgh

The Sun

You remind me of a frisbee flying through the blue sky
You remind me of an egg yolk mingling between the clouds
At night your other half shows shining our way through the night
Like a crowd of people congregating in a town centre.

Luke Smith (12)
Hermitage Academy, Helensburgh

The Sun

The eye of the sun is shining bright
Shining oh a beautiful light
Shining down on me and you
So we can do what we want to do
You show us the way
All through the day
But when the night is dawning
The sun starts yawning
And when it is dark and the stories are read
It is time for the sun to go to bed.

Catriona Dolan (13)
Hermitage Academy, Helensburgh

World Around Me

When I felt the wind against my face
I suddenly realised I was in the human race
I saw the sun hanging high above
Its fiery power that I so love.

The world around me keeps spinning around
The light bounces from the ground
I hear the birds singing in the sky
It sounds like their sweet merry cry.

I love the sound of the gentle wind
It blows my mind straight through the wind
The sun goes down, it's time to go
See you later, I've got to go.

Mhairi Hanlon (12)
Hermitage Academy, Helensburgh

An English Lesson To Remember

As I sit on the ground and breathe in the air
The world grows around me as I sit and stare
At the gardens and buildings that stand everywhere
On this beautiful breezy afternoon.

As the blackbird calls his cheerful song
Like my stereo's been brought outside
And the tree blossoms in full bloom
And I smell its fragrance, I smile.

The sun is so bright like a big bulging light
That burns in the sky, all day, all night
It shines down upon me and keeps me going this peaceful day
That makes the chatter of children seem so far away.

As the butterfly lands like a bird on the wind
And the flowers sway, I sit here
Writing my poem for my English competition.

Lauren Carruthers (12)
Hermitage Academy, Helensburgh

A Curious Mind

Blue eyes full of wonder, staring at the sky
Could everyone be wrong, could we possibly fly?
Do you ever ponder the meaning of a word?
Why can it be spoken? Why can it be heard?
Would you notice me if I stood up in a crowd?
What if that crowd was silent and I said something out loud?
What if I told you I'm from a different race?
Would you stop and stare? Would you frown at me in disgrace?
Don't let people tell you what you can and cannot do
Make your own decisions, make your dreams come true
Is it really necessary to make fun of the deaf, the mute and the blind?
All of these are thoughts and questions of a strangely curious mind.

Nadine Royle (13)
Hermitage Academy, Helensburgh

Nature's Game

You remind me of a football flying through the sky
Like a really high punt
The wind like a football crowd shouting
The goals like hills when the ball goes over
The blue sky never-ending
The moon like the ref keeping control of the game
The wind blows, the crowd is shouting
The clouds have scored.

Brad Lamington (13)
Hermitage Academy, Helensburgh

On This Sunny Day

One sunny day the birds were singing
Church bells ringing on this sunny day.

Clouds floating like giant marshmallows
In the deep blue sky
A kite will fly on this sunny day.

The children run and dance, across the lake
They like to prance on this sunny day.

The beach is golden, the sand is molten
Cool water on my ankles on this sunny day.

I see the ferry, getting closer
Like a giant killer whale, on this sunny day.

So now the day is over, everyone has gone
Even though the fun has just begun, on this sunny day.

Rebecca Watson (12)
Hermitage Academy, Helensburgh

Beautifully Pure

You hang in the sky
Like a great ball of light
But you disappear sadly at night.

You creep and you crawl
And you don't speak at all
If I dropped you a long way, you'd fall.

You shimmer and shine
You look so divine
I wish you were mine.

You glide through the air
With no worms to spare
And feathers, no hair.

In winter you look so dead and dreary
Your leaves are broken, your trunk is weary
But in spring, you come alive
And all your pretty buds arrive.

You drift along in the sky
Nobody knows how you can fly
Fluffy, white, black or grey
You're way up high there every day.

The world is beautiful in most ways
We should all appreciate the days
When the sun is out, the sky is blue
The world is bright for me and you.

Kirsty Pristaw (12)
Hermitage Academy, Helensburgh

Remembrance

With bombs the street is full
And wreckage fills the air
The sirens blast their warning
With screaming and despair.

In the cold and dirt
The trenches they all stand
While everything around
Explodes and fades to sand.

Now there's nothing left
Was it real at all?
In their place just poppies
And rain like teardrops fall.

A poppy for those silent
One minute every year
A poppy for each memory
A poppy for each tear.

A poppy for each solider
Who fought to save our lives
A poppy for those weeping
For sons and lovers died.

Ella Mackay (12)
Hermitage Academy, Helensburgh

Shoals

We swim from side to side and left to right
Our movements go in unison
We dance and prance from place to place
Our movements are in harmony.

And all at once our movements change
There's danger in the air
A predator moves and comes to life
As he spots his tea tonight
We move, he follows
Faster, faster, faster, faster,
Faster, faster, *strike!*

Slowly our form recreates
Half the size it once was
The predator has made his strike
And had his meal
We are safe, but not for long.

We gently move from side to side
In unison once more
Our colours shine
As our shape reforms and twists
From side to side.

Our journey has no end
For we never stop
For we never wait
Because life is underwater.

Harry Crumless (12)
Hermitage Academy, Helensburgh

Laugh And Cry

The warning siren sounds
People hurry to shelters buried underground
Under mounds of rubble people lie dead
Blood seeps from wounds in their heads.

As we hide down under the chapel
Men get blown to bits by shrapnel
We hear their dying cry
Which fills the dangerous sky.

As fighting in the sky becomes scarier
The home guard patrol the area
Women laugh and cry
As their children and lovers live and die.

Women hold their children tight
As men sign up to fight
The cities are no longer safe
All we can do is keep our faith.

Rosemary Jennings-Maun (12)
Hermitage Academy, Helensburgh

Gooner

As the ball hits the back of the net
The crowd rises as one and falls as one
As if somehow they are connected.

Whether you're at the stadium, watching it on the telly
Listening to it on the radio or just being told about it by a mate
There is an immense pride of being a *gooner*.

To wear the proud red and white shirt
You know you're part of something great
To shout the name of the players as they're shouted to you by the tannoy
You get the feeling of being at one with the club.

To roar the players on to victory
Or to get that goal
To clinch the match is something special.

It can make you feel high enough to touch the sky
Or it can make you feel lower than the ground
This is the magic of being a *gooner*.

To be with the club as it goes on a winning streak
Or to support it when you are going through a bad patch in the season
To celebrate and go delirious with joy
Or sit quietly and mourn about everything that went wrong.

It might not sound great
But that's the head and tails of the matter
I wouldn't swap to support any other team in the world.

You can keep your Man United and your big stars
Because at Arsenal you feel different to anywhere else
And that's the brilliant thing that makes football fans everywhere
Completely the same.

David Pellow (14)
Hermitage Academy, Helensburgh

My Sister

I have a little sister, her name is Isla Joan
She is quite smart and she lives with us at home
She gives us a fright in the night when she wakes
And cries when she's tired the very next day.

She gets very mucky during the day
After all the working and playing away
But after her bath, she's a beautiful girl
Ready for bed with a little kiss curl.

Her favourite toy is her beddy bear
Which she takes to bed and cuddles near
During the day she loves to be outside
She plays on her bike and her swing and her slide.

She loves her food and would eat it all day
If Mum and Dad let her have her own way
She eats very healthily most of the time
But after some treats, she then feels fine.

Everybody thinks my sister is lovely
Because she is cute and very bubbly
I love my sister and she loves me
She is the centre of our family.

Sophie Finn (12)
Hermitage Academy, Helensburgh

Candy Land

As I wished beside the wishing well
I wished for stories I could tell
I dreamed of living in a chocolate land
With trees that grew from sugar strands
I built a house from gingerbread
With soft marshmallows for my bed
There was icing on the mountain tops
And rain that fell in lemon drops
Clouds of candyfloss in the sky
Colourful sugar mice scampering by
Fizzy fish swim in a caramel stream
Topped with waves of fresh whipped cream
An endless stretch of sherbet sand
I'd like to live in this strange land
Still dreaming by the wishing well
I thought this land would be a dentist's hell.

David Reid (12)
Hermitage Academy, Helensburgh

Music

Birds do not sing sweeter
Than the sound of your wondrous notes
At home you are the joker
But in concert you are the king
You can be as silent as a mouse
Or as loud as an elephant
You can be as slow as a tortoise
Strolling through the garden
You can be as fast as a cheetah
Darting towards the prey
You can make us dance, laugh and sing
Of our ears and hearts you are our king.

Alison West (12)
Hermitage Academy, Helensburgh

Help, My Brother's A Doctor Who Fanatic!

Help, my brother's a Doctor Who fanatic
He's got lots of Who magazines stored up in the attic
He watches every episode
He never misses one
He watches them *so* much he never gets anything else done
His favourite monsters are the Daleks
He really is a 'Smart Alec'
Don't let him get started on the Cybermen
He'll watch them over and over again
And then there's the Slitheen, oh it makes me turn green
When I see him watching Doctor Who again, it's obscene
But the one thing he just doesn't stop talking about
No, not the Daleks, the Cybermen or even the Slitheen
Why, it's the Doctor of course, and the little blue *TARDIS!*

Sarah Bonthrone (12)
Hermitage Academy, Helensburgh

I Hate Mondays

I wake up early in the morning and look at the calendar . . .
Darn, it's Monday, I hate Mondays
The sun is splitting the sky when I remembered . . .
Darn, it's Monday, I hate Mondays
I get through school in one piece
And everything goes well, but . . .
Darn, it's Monday, I hate Mondays
Then I get home and I start to enjoy myself with my mates yet . . .
Darn, it's Monday, I hate Mondays
I go to bed and wake up next morning . . .
Darn, it's Tuesday . . .

Callum Downs (12)
Hermitage Academy, Helensburgh

Sun, Sea And Sky

As blue as the sea on a picturesque day
And the sun beats down along the way
It looks like I could jump in like it's the sea
And swim along so easily.

A single cloud hangs in the air
And the birds fly along, not a worry or a care
Scarlet dragonflies dance around the pool
And overhead the sky looks so dazzling and cool.

As I look across the sea
And the ships sail along quite peacefully
As the sand burns my feet I sit and think
How nice it would be to just drift off to sleep.

Laura McGhie (13)
Hermitage Academy, Helensburgh

The Silent Girl

Some say she is walking
Some even say she is talking
She walks along the lonely street
She passes me every morning
I ask her what her name is
She ignores me more and more.

She walks and talks
But nobody can hear her
When I ask her anything you should see her face
She just runs off at a steady pace.

I worry that she has no friends
No family and home
She wanders round the town at night
Standing all alone
How sad it is to see her pay for her mother's accident.

When I went to see her
One cold stormy night
Just to see if she had a home
Or somewhere for the night
Her face was pale, her body was stiff
She had a fallen smile
Her face was covered in tears and rain
How sad it is to see her pay for her mother's accident.

She is always outside, never goes back home
Or where she used to live
Her mother must live somewhere
Or her father who is never seen
How sad it is to see her pay for her mother's accident.

Jasna Wardle (13)
Hermitage Academy, Helensburgh

A Sense Of Place

I felt good when I arrived at this place
But everyone's staring at me
Even though we are the same race.

People fear me, they don't come near me
I haven't done any crimes
But I still haven't changed the way you see me.

Everyone's looking, I don't know what I did
Turns out they're looking at me because I'm big.

I felt great, that was before I arrived
But now I feel I might not survive.

They gave me chilling looks like they were gonna slay me
At first I ignored them, but now it's driving me crazy.

Everyone's saying how much they love this place
I couldn't comprehend
Everyone thinks it's nice
But if you look closer, all you see are poor men.

Now looks they don't bother me
I thought I had problems, these people living in poverty.

If you don't know this place, never go alone
You could end up lost or never going home.

Atif Riaz (15)
Hermitage Academy, Helensburgh

The Ghost Of Lanmark Hall

In a mysterious hall
In a mysterious house
I saw the face of a girl
It was white with a chill
That sent shivers down my back
As the moon shone brightly in
Some people don't believe me
They say that I am mad
But I know that that girl exists
The ghost of Lanmark Hall.

She wears a dark brown shawl
That she found in an old church hall
She gazes up at the stars
Like sugar in the sky
She lets her hair grow 10 metres long
It trails along wherever she goes
Trailing on through time
The ghost of Lanmark Hall.

They say she has no family
That they left when she was young
They left a red cross on the door
And fled to save their souls
The plague caught up and she was killed
The ghost of Lanmark Hall.

Gillian Allan (13)
Hermitage Academy, Helensburgh

Memories

There used to be the days when you go around with your shoes off
Your feet digging in at all the jaggy stones that pierce your feet.

Those were days when the Spice Girls were the best thing on Earth
And the biggest pain you had was scraping your knee.

When the only things boys could break were your toys
You always used to obey your teachers as they had the knowledge
                                                       of the world.

Those were the weekends that you spent mainly with your family
                                            and went for picnics

And you knew they were *always* right.

When you look at the memories that you've had since you were
                                            no taller than a chair
The memories of when school was great and jelly shoes
                                            were worn 24/7.

Those are the memories of wee girls who wish they could go back
And stay that way forever.

Christine McKelvie (14)
Hermitage Academy, Helensburgh

Love Poem

Love is rare
Love is not fair
Love is found when you are around
When love comes, take it, take it
Don't mistake it
Young love is cute
Old love is sweet
Broken hearts can't be mended
When love is broken
Falling in love is like a new beginning
The words *I love you* just keep spinning round your head.

Ashleigh Milnes (13)
Hermitage Academy, Helensburgh

A Sense Of Place

The run-down barn at the end of the lane, full of childhood memories
Covered in cobwebs and dust, waiting to be found.

House martins soaring in and out, carrying things in their beaks
Building a nest and feeding their young.

Surrounded by trees, old and new
The ground littered with leaves and branches covered in moss.

Opposite the barn is a wide green field
The sheep graze on the grass and a hawk circles overhead
                                        searching for prey.

This is my garden, my favourite place in the world
With cats running amok and swings swaying in the breeze.

A view of Loch Long with boats going by
Yet everything is peaceful and still . . .

Then a cat starts to yowl and a bird starts to sing
The silence has disappeared but will return soon.

Rosanagh Watson (15)
Hermitage Academy, Helensburgh

A Few Problems

As I look out the window I contemplate the world
The sun shines on the mountains, the crystal-blue loch glitters
                                                    like gems
The trees sway gently in the warm wind
But I am not fooled, I hear cars screaming past
Their black gunge bellows out, the grass lies dead
A tarmac monster rips them apart
A warm world becomes a fireball
Far away on a desert plain . . . an explosion
A guttural cry of pain, hundreds dead
Millions injured, cruel men play cruel games
Death and destruction, all hidden under the banner of religion
When I'm home I think nearer
                        A woman dying
There is a spark of hope
                        An ambulance on the way
But too long it takes
                        The hospital no longer there
Her eyes darken
                        The spark dampened
She rests now
                        Eternal rest
Not all the world is despair
                        There is still green grass
And yellow flowers
                        Scents and sounds
Like waterfalls
        But
                The world does have
                    A few problems.

Simon Anderson (15)
Hermitage Academy, Helensburgh

A Sense Of Place

There are names and faces
And fame in famous places
Glamour and class pour throughout the streets
And the sun shines over the rising stars of tomorrow.

The young and beautiful strut down the boulevard
In the vain hope that they'll be noticed
And see their name up in lights
Their faces on every newspaper and magazine
Followed and spoken about in every cafe and shop they enter and exit.

This is the place that dreams are made of.

And you can't help but feel famous in such a place
Even with the tacky tourist shops surrounding you
When you walk down the star-lined streets
With your oversized designer sunglasses, tanned legs and high-heels
You feel good, you feel famous.

And when your dad wants to take a family photo
You can't resist the temptation to strike a pose
And put on a superstar smile
And pretend it's the paparazzi photographing you
You truly believe that all eyes are on you
After all, this is no place to be camera shy.

But then you tilt your sunglasses back on top of your head and see . . .
Beggars sit lifeless on every corner
The cheap and tacky shops surround you
Far from anything you've ever seen in the movies
You crash back down to Earth
And see that with the beautiful and glamorous
Comes the rundown and ugly
Even in Hollywood . . .

Amy Thomas (14)
Hermitage Academy, Helensburgh

Through The Gate/Escape

I take one step and cross the threshold of the gate
I am gazing onto an emerald ocean
As I walk through the mildew-covered grass
The forest awaits
I breathe in the sweet scent of the morning
I am alive
Through bracken and brambles I trudge
Knowing that my reward will be just
To the daunting face of relentless rock I arrive
Waiting for me just before my goal
I can see the opening in the dense forest, the reward
I want just beyond my reach
So over the face of rock I climb
A perilous journey that will be worth it in the end
As I take the last step and clear the face
A gaze over the horizon, and I am startled

I move to the place I once stood as a child
And my jaw drops
The lake at the bottom of the hill
Where the sun once reflected its golden rays onto the sea of pine trees
Is now a barren desert of scorched mud
The reeds where birds once nestled and squirrels once played
Now a patch of fine scorched earth
My sanctuary now little more than a dump

I rub my eyes in disbelief
The one place I would go to release my personal fears and just not
                                                    have to care
My exit, my escape, used now for little more than a few houses built
                                                    for profit

So I turn and I walk
I don't care where I end up
I go over a small hill and realise that all is not lost
I will search and when I am finished I will find my new sanctuary
My new place of rest
My new escape.

Sam Stacey (14)
Hermitage Academy, Helensburgh

Crumpling World

O' beautiful world, where we live
We treat this world like it is nothing
But we must remember that it is our mother, our protector
If we keep killing the Earth
There will be no turning back
Then we will have nowhere to go
Unless we change our ways
Our home will become a desolate waste of space
Our oceans will become polluted deathtraps
And our trees will be cut down and their rich soil will become harsh lifeless plains
Wildlife will struggle to cope with rapidly changing landscapes
But this isn't far in the future, it's happening now.

Struan Wylie (12)
Hermitage Academy, Helensburgh

My Heart In Pain

How come in my dreams I see your face
And when I see you in school you don't care?
How come you look at me for a second then look away
And I ask you something, you look away and leave me alone?
So how come in my dream you're my Prince Charming
But in real life you have your princess and I'm the sad one here?
So how come when I think of you my heart is in pain?
One thing I have learned is that love is hard to live with
And I will never forget your face
Because I believe in true love
And no one can take that away from me.

Megan Macaulay (14)
Hermitage Academy, Helensburgh

Flight Of A Soul

The cool rain soothes my burning skin, mixes with my hot tears
Twilight smothers me with its shimmering gold glow
Shadows . . . dancing, flitting like swallows in flight
Crimson sky and violet clouds melt into the distance
Darkness creeps up behind me like a great bat, shielding the Earth
                                                     with its leathery wings
Stars, pinpricked holes in the fabric of the universe
The night swallows me with its silky black folds
And my soul leaps out to moonbathe on a star.

Holly Muir (12)
Hermitage Academy, Helensburgh

Tortoise

T iny and small
O r big but not tall
R aspberries and strawberries
T ortoises aren't very keen on cherries
O ver the rocks
I n a big glass box
S lowly, slowly over the ground
E verybody thinks they're hard to be found.

Stephanie Carpenter (12)
Hermitage Academy, Helensburgh

Earth's End

The Earth is spinning round as normal as it goes
Though it's all about to change but no one on it knows
The people sitting normally doing normal things
The blackbird it is in the tree, we listen as it sings.

Then it happened . . .

The ice walls started getting thick and then began to sink
The sea was ever rising and the world began to think
The Earth we saw in green and blue was then almost covered in sea
The animals started drowning causing all the rest to flee.

The wind howled through the leaning trees like a lone wolf on a cliff
Everything we thought was fake we knew then was not a myth
Fires started breaking out all across the world
Earthquakes started shaking out, meteors were hurled.

Everyone was screaming now, the birds had stopped their songs
We thought the world would never end, but we knew we were wrong
So let this be a warning, to save the world while you can
Everyone can help, each and every man.

Carly Trille (12)
Hermitage Academy, Helensburgh

My Dog

My dog is very big
He likes to play tig
He's black and white
He's never out of sight
I love my dog
Even though he's a ball hog
He loves his soft toy
But he can be such a bad boy
We teach him tricks
And when we feed him he has dry mix
I like to give him a big hug
But when I walk him he can really tug
When I give him a brush
He goes and walks through a big bush
He makes us feel safe and sound
This is good for a four-legged hound
When we say, let's go to the park
He sets off with a big bark.

Rebecca Hamer (12)
Hermitage Academy, Helensburgh

My Pet Budgie

I have a pet budgie called Joey
And he lives in a cage made from wood
He poos a lot for a budgie
But then he eats a lot of food!

He has golden feathers and a blue beak
When he opens his mouth he makes a loud squeak
We let him out sometimes to help stretch his wings
But he eats my mum's plants and a lot of other things.

Joey's a boy, so I taught him to talk
Now he says, 'Pretty boy Joey'
When we let him out, he doesn't fly, he walks
And sometimes he listens to David Bowie!

Harry Cotton (12)
Hermitage Academy, Helensburgh

Football Crazy

Footballs are white and shin pads are grey
The fields are green and the crowd is blue, so are you

I watch you kick the ball far away
And I find out how you play
I wish I could play like you
Believe me it's true.

You can play all day
And not get tired
Believe me you would *never* get fired
You're great, you're great, you're great!

You kick balls all over green fields
And you would never need shields

I see you, I see you
Goodbye for now
Give a fantastic smile
And give a great bow!

Frank Mulholland (13)
Hermitage Academy, Helensburgh

The Noise

Static bursts when the cable slams into the socket
Reflecting on the jet-black body of the guitar
The amp snarls when the first chords ring out
Shattering noise like a banshee's scream
Resonating against the walls of the room.

They shake with the brutal grumble
My hand hold loosens up and down the neck
A volley of notes rips into my fingers.

The feedback mounts, the volume rises
Eventually pushing the limits
When a blunt shout from another room thumps
I'll give them quiet
Silence until the next time.

Ross Cameron (13)
Islay High School, Bowmore

Seanair
(Gaelic for Grandfather)

I remember everyone being on mute
The rain was tap, tap, tapping on the windows
Black suits enveloped me, shiny
Black shoes replacing muddy green wellie boots.

There was crying, tears, wet
Tissues. The church filling up
With friends, family
Some strangers.

Then the coffin, smothered
With cheery flowers
Why, I thought, *were flowers so happy?*
Why did their sweet scent have to roam
The church like music?

I remember him perfectly
Conjuring sweet chewy toffee
From sugar over the fire
My Seanair sitting in his blue overalls
And flat cap.

Lucy Darroch (13)
Islay High School, Bowmore

Winter

A sparkling blanket of white
Covers the soon to be shoots of spring
A translucent sheet of crystals
Hides the deep blue loch's community.

The full moon beams down
Like a pearl in the night sky
Creating shifty shadows
Between the trees of the forest.

An owl hoots
As an icicle, tinkling, falls
And the serenity of this winter night
Returns calm.

Anna Storrie (14)
Islay High School, Bowmore

Spain

I went to Spain on holiday
What a lovely time
I met some Spanish people with medium tanned skin
Spanish music, Spanish food and Spanish dancing
Summer music filled the air
Balmy evenings, not a care
Holiday in Spain memories forever.

Kerry Gibson (19)
Knockevin Special School, Downpatrick

Football

My school pals and I
Went on a football trip to Belfast
We ran up and down the pitch
We tried to score goals
But hit the post much more
The opposition were much better at scoring
So that left us roaring!

Lisa Stewart (16)
Knockevin Special School, Downpatrick

Dreams

Memories are precious
They are like jewels
They help us out when we are sad
They help us get over the bad.

Dreams help us to fulfil
All the things that we want to do
To accomplish what might be
To prove to the world our destiny.

Charlene Anderson (19)
Knockevin Special School, Downpatrick

Ballet Lessons

I went to ballet lessons
When I was young
They were happy times
First I was a bit nervous
But when I started dancing
My fears melted away
I was wearing my tutu
I was a wee girl
I remember I was twirling
I felt very light and dreamy
Those were happy days.

Clare Orr (18)
Knockevin Special School, Downpatrick

Tidewater

I go to Tidewater
Beside the sea.
It's a cosy little café
It's work for me.
I see Mary and Briget
I do dishes and the drinks cabinet.
My friends came in to say hello.
It's such a happy time for me.

Ruairi Armstrong (18)
Knockevin Special School, Downpatrick

Come Home
(This poem is dedicated to Madeleine McCann)

Come home Madeleine
We hope and pray
You are so young
Please don't stay away.

You are only four
And your brother and sister miss you
It will break our hearts
To see you no more.

It's your birthday on Saturday
No card or cake
We light a candle to God
To bring you home
And keep you safe.

Shannon Lawlor (12)
Our Lady of Mercy Girls' School, Belfast

End Of The School Year

Everyone is screaming
Books are in the bin
I'm having trouble understanding
By the way my name is Tim.

I have asked my new friend Robbie
And also asked old Jim
But I still don't understand it
Not one little bit
When I checked my diary
It's the end of the school year!

Connor Barrass (13)
St Saviour's High School, Dundee

Winter!

Winter is . . .
The time for singing
With church bells ringing
There can be some glittery lights
With sparkling sights.

Winter is . . .
The time for ripping
With snowflakes dripping
And snowy white snowmen
With sledges of snow.

Winter is . . .
The time for ice
You may get some mice
They will be freezing cold
With no place to go.

Winter is . . .
The time for sleet
You will have freezing feet
Remember to wrap up the gifts
Open up the bubbly and listen to the rifts.

Amy Miller (13)
St Saviour's High School, Dundee

True Love

One day ends another starts new
Longing for the one day I see you
I can't go anywhere without thinking of you
Still I wait for days on end
Hoping for my true love to mend
My broken heart again.

Rebekah Sommerville (13)
St Saviour's High School, Dundee

Multicolour

Red is the colour of our school tie
Blue is the colour of the beautiful clear sky
Green is the colour of the bright dry grass
Yellow is the colour of the sun from up above
Purple is the colour of the Ribena you drink at lunch
Orange is the colour of the amber on the traffic light
Pink is the colour of my favourite skirt
Silver is the colour of the beautiful half moon
Gold is the colour of my diamond ring
Black is the colour of the dark night sky.

Amber McIver (13)
St Saviour's High School, Dundee

I Miss You

When I need you
You're not there
When I see you
It's hard to bear.

You went away
And broke my heart
Now you're with her
It's hard not to start.

You've changed so much
In such little time
Now I feel like
You're not even mine.

You used to say
Your life was bad
But please remember
You're still my dad.

Ciara McCluskey (14)
St Saviour's High School, Dundee

Thoughts Of Love

Every minute you are sad
Every day when life is bad
Think of happy thoughts
The good times you have had.

I think the thoughts
I cry so hard
I wish you'd never left me this way
It feels like it was only yesterday.

I try to move on
But I don't know how
At this moment
I wish I was higher than the clouds.

You said you loved me
I said I loved you
When I sneezed
You said, 'Bless you.'

I don't know what to say
I don't know what to do
I still love you
I wish you loved me too.

Every minute you are sad
Every day when life is bad
Think of happy thoughts
The good times you have had.

Demi-Louise Simpson (14)
St Saviour's High School, Dundee

The Shadow

Darkness here lives the shadow
Long, dark and black
The shadow creeping up to the window
Peering, standing on the dark sack.

Scraping, scratching in the midnight moon
Creeping, crawling in the city's grass
Sunlight will be shining soon
Windows slamming as it walks past.

The night is its friend
Clenching the dripping knife
Going to mend as he walked the bend
Not the same as his past life.

A favour for Death
The final job
To take away his breath
Wring his neck, his wife will sob.

Grabbing the door
Breaking in its hands
His neck will be sore
Blood dripping in the pans.

Lee Gillespie (14)
St Saviour's High School, Dundee

Absent Thoughts

Even thought you are gone, you're always on my mind
It's been four years now and I still want to hide
When you died it confused me
How can such a great woman make me so blue?

Then I realised it wasn't down to you
God saw you getting weary and knew what to do
Sadly, a cure was not to be
So He gently whispered in your ear, 'Come with me.'

Kelly Hunter (14)
St Saviour's High School, Dundee

The Horrors Of War

Away from home and stuck in the trenches,
Not used to all the smells and stenches,
Bullets flying and the bombshells dropping,
Rain is falling and the puddles are plopping.

Waiting for the word of command,
We ready ourselves with weapons in hand,
To attack the army of the Axis nation,
Fighting in our desperation.

Side by side the 1st Battalion
Charging like an angry stallion
Victory is our only chance
Crush our enemies with a final glance.

Hand to hand, eye to eye
Some of us live and others may die
Grenades, guns, even knives
Will help us smash our Axis strife.

Fighting for country and even Queen
The blood and the gore which I have seen
Six years of war and hate
We work hard and fire straight.

Hitler's army is full of might
But we attack in the dead of night
Once it is finished, it is never more
These all are the horrors of war.

James Mitchell (13)
St Saviour's High School, Dundee

Music

Music is what makes the world go round,
Music is what turns my frown upside down.
Music helps me through the good and the bad,
Whenever I hear music I can *never* be sad.

Darlene Paxton (13)
St Saviour's High School, Dundee

My Secret Garden

It's my place to escape -
Escape from my thundering troubles
The breeze calms my nerves
Is pleasing to my eyes.

The grass has never been cut
Butterflies fly high over my face
The bird's nest has never been invaded
Baby buttercups sway with grace.

Ladybirds creep over my skin
While I lie there dreaming
I don't want to go now
My dream hasn't ended.

I'll stay for another few hours
Letting my hair wisp in the air
Skimming stones through the pond
Watching the ripples in the water.

Suzannah Dunn (14)
Shimna Integrated College, Newcastle

Happiness

I'm like a gleeful elephant
Flopping around in a lake.

I'm like a cup of hot chocolate
Spilling over the cup.

I'm like a newborn baby
Ready to explore life.

I'm like a million years
Of a lifetime.

Nina Graham (13)
Shimna Integrated College, Newcastle

A Boy Nicknamed Rat

Grey, but runs like a flash of light
Long, pink, spiky tail
Hides in the smallest places
That you can't even think of
You hear, *squeak, squeak*
In the morning
It's like a fluffy alarm clock
It looks at you with hatred
Never walks in a line -
Always zigzags.

Elaine Kelly (14)
Shimna Integrated College, Newcastle

As Free As A Bird

Whenever I am walking my dog
Being towed along
I look up through the overgrown trees
Up into the big blue sky
And watch all the birds fly past
So happy and free
Soaring, playing with their friends
It's just lovely to watch them having fun
Not caring about the world below them.

Kathryn Curry (14)
Shimna Integrated College, Newcastle

I Was Free As A Tree

I am a tree
I felt as if I were free
The wind was my friend
And now it howls at me
It hurts me day in, day out
I cry with agony
When children climb up me
A scream
Of horror comes from
Within
I know something will fall
But what?
A branch? A bird's nest
Or a three-year-old child?

Gordon Donaldson (14)
Shimna Integrated College, Newcastle

The Warp

As I marched onto the shadow plain
I could feel the dead's fear
All those soldiers slaughtered and slain
I knew I shouldn't be here.

The stench of death was in the air
I could hear the wounded cry
The ashes of death fluttered in my hair
The hate of the Persians so sly.

I sensed the enemy over the hill
As I drew my sword from its scabbard
Their mission to seek and to kill
So I told my men to assemble and charge.

Metals crashed and flesh burned
For the cost of war we pay the price
Those who die must take their turns
My comrades dead, the feeling not nice.

Now we know the price of war
No longer does battle seem fun
Now we know the pain of war
Fighting for me in battle is done.

David Mawhirt (14)
Shimna Integrated College, Newcastle

Fear

I stand in the end of the woods
Staring into the meadow
It looks nice and calm
But I can feel in my hooves there is danger
I want to run, but I don't
I feel scared and nervous
My legs are shaking
Then it is all quiet
And there is a bang
And I don't see anything after that.

Kirsty Smyth (14)
Shimna Integrated College, Newcastle

Natasha

My little niece is such a cutie
She always gives me a smile
When I go in, she runs towards me.

Her favourite food is 'nanas
And apples, all mushed up
She covers me in goo when I pick her up.

She loves going for walks
She hates when I talk
She loves pushing her buggy instead of being in it.

She is my little honey bunny
I'll always love her, no matter what she does
If she pukes, I'll love her, even if it's on me
She'll always be my sweetie.

Jane McEvoy (13)
Shimna Integrated College, Newcastle

Reduce, Re-Use, Recycle - Haiku

Re-use milk cartons
Amounts of rubbish will shrink
Reclaim and salvage.

Matt Boyle (14)
Shimna Integrated College, Newcastle

Masks

A man going to work,
a teenager caught smoking,
a young girl playing in snow.

A student graduating,
a footballer scoring,
a widow going through woe.

A kid getting bullied,
an adult fired,
a toddler running to hide.

Someone is racist,
a teenager fighting,
two cars about to collide.

A bank being robbed,
an Orangeman marches,
a riot about to start.

A rugby team loses,
a teardrop falls,
two friends are going to part.

John Nellis (13)
Shimna Integrated College, Newcastle

Eagle

It soars so silently,
the only thing you can hear
is its screams for food.

Its sharp, deadly black eyes
just glaring at you
like it's going to attack you.

It circles an area
casting a shadow over the bare ground.
One minute the ground is packed
with animals and insects
then a shadow appears on the ground
and everyone scatters.

Its back is so lovely and soft
with lovely patterns:
but its beak is a deadly sharp weapon
and its claws like knives.

Brian Nelson (14)
Shimna Integrated College, Newcastle

Sectarianism

Why are we fighting?
Protestant or Catholic
We're all equal
No need to be psychopathic

Sectarianism has gone too far
On this Gracious Land
Let's all be friends
And have sectarianism banned!

Put our differences aside
Too much blood has been spilled
Too many innocent people
Have been killed

Let's all be friends
Put the memories to the past
One thing is all I ask
Be at peace at last.

Naill McAnallen (14)
Shimna Integrated College, Newcastle

In Dhaka's Fields

It was to be a surprise, so it was, but it turned out not
Not for the worse, but for the better
The vast field was meant to lie in ruins
Or at least that's what the Marni's had planned
But nature decided to take its toll.

As the terrain was soaked, the rubble crumbled
The blustery winds shook the entire field
Decimating the entire area and causing the planned attack to be cancelled
The wind was the cause and the Marni's paid the price.

The Lacki's were lucky on that stormy day
They were meant to be the victims of a brutal attack
But it was the attackers that suffered
After nature's terrible storm came to a close
The Marni's were the laughing-stocks in the end.

Ryan McCallum (14)
Stonelaw High School, Rutherglen

You Keep Me Standing

Remember our Thursdays? Our street-wandering Thursdays
Over the bridge painted like a chipped and dirtied sky
With people who'll fade in and out of focus every year.

Faces upturned, our eyes follow the breeze
Building palaces from white clouds and spring sunshine
Forging dreams and forgetting them all at once.

Remember my garden? Bare feet on warm stone,
The sun-washed wooden den where we sat behind the door
As we smiled in the lazy shadows of summer.

White moths shivered from blade to blade
Pale ghosts in the shining grass of my garden
A grave stands there now.

Remember the wood pigeon on the fence?
It was soft grey against the rest of the autumn sky
Soft call against the harsh scream of train tracks.

Something in its eyes stopped me
Do you remember? I stopped and I wondered
We never saw it fly, but the next day it was gone.

Remember the warmth of the china mugs?
We both held them in shivering fingers
And watched snowflakes fill our footsteps outside.

You let me in and I sat on the piano stool
Before the Christmas tree that glowed like Heaven
Or was that just my imagination?

You're the one who keeps me standing, and
Sometimes you're a friend, sister or someone I can't recall
And sometimes the grave in the garden is yours.

Remember the New Year? I was so glad to see it
After lying dead in hospital only months before
I know you got me back on my feet.

Julie Smith (13)
Stonelaw High School, Rutherglen

Criminal Mind

I used to have a criminal mind
But I changed just in time
Cos the day I saw a boy get knifed
I thought I would have to change my criminal mind.

In the past I was a bad wee boy
But since I have been in Kibble my life is changed
It didn't change quick, it didn't change fast
But in the end I turned out good at last.

Jordan King (15)
The Kibble School, Paisley

Adalia

Start again.

A woman like a diamond field
With dust and dirt footprints over
Will dull the sparkle from her smile
For men to harvest for sale
A profit she will never see.

Now gems that once glittered bright
Won't now reflect the glare of morning light
For all the beauty she possessed
Would not live for more than our amusement.

Start again.

Pick a brand new name
Meek as who she wants to be
And vanish to where they will let flowers grow
Not cut and tie nature for a living
Their living
Vanish to where she will be the only woman
Not the other woman in another triangle
Among the trees where she will be at peace
With polka music playing from distant shows -
Judged by character and not by clothes . . .
And she will have reason to dance
As she receives her second chance.

Vanessa Ifediora (17)
Victoria College, Belfast

Moments

Everything's waiting for me, ready and new
The paper so white, fresh - clean.
The pencil, prepared to the perfect point - not too blunt or sharp.
The only thing that's left unready is I. My ideas
All the old, used up thoughts swirl in the back of my mind
They'd only contaminate the perfect page.
Because now is the moment
When I'm supposed to think of something fantastically original
Something never seen before
Something to charm each and every adjudicator -
But my imagination must be in hibernation
Because I can think of nothing to blunt the pencil
No thought worthy of the prestigiously white paper
Now that moment has passed
And it's too late to charm anyone.

Shannon Magnano (14)
Victoria College, Belfast

Blame It On The Rain

Against the windowpane
Shatters, tiny droplets of joy
The desolate air, once warm and sweet
Is humming with a more foreboding scent
And all at once my heart
      Jumps
At the thought of your touch
That left me so long ago
The tear-tracked reflection in the stormy
Mirror, changing vastly
With the coming season yet holding tightly
      What has past.

As the tea steams and the ink stains
I sit quiet. Holding the last memory alive.
Holding you alive in my mind.

Nicola Woods (17)
Victoria College, Belfast

Pictures Of Paris

Pictures of Paris, glistening city
Lights that smacked me off my delighted feet
The self-reliant stranger, slowly swinging
Shoes too high on the right, left hand grappling
With that elusive banister of golden air
Stumbling my way to the Sorbonne. We're
Laughing - I forget why, some mistranslated joke perhaps -
I choked on my smile, the bandage slipped, then
You stole my heels. Is there a singular? For it was only one
Two of a kind but one of a pair across the Pont Neuf
De nuit, c'est beau . . . our reckless minds
Intoxicated by exoneration's sweet liqueurs
Freewheeling towards the Rue Dauphine
Winding through arrows on a map we lost.
I watch you hurl my beloved shoe
(That poor cat had somehow offended you
On the shadowy corner of the Rue Hautefeuille)
And demanded compensation. It didn't matter -
You picked it up and swung me, giggling
Over your shoulder. I heard the phones ring
And the boulevard bells blossomed into stars
Brightly white and madly unrevealing -
I didn't care. Just as long as one of us
Knew where we were going.

Tonight, I am not coming home.
I hold the images in my palm and
I hunger for it, the chance to again,
Seek 'les aventures sauvages' in darkness
Save the world through muddled contemplation
Tripping on our
Tongues and sense of direction.

Emma Lui (17)
Victoria College, Belfast

Ross

I see you
Lying on the bed
Fighting
Against the slippery rocks of life.
The machines light up and bleep;
Mini lighthouses
Trying to warn you of death.

I walk away
Crying
Knowing that you could be
Wrecked
On the rocks of life.
You could slip
Through my fingers
Onto the beach
And be washed away
To the endless pit
Of the sea.

Kieran Gibson (12)
Wellington School, Ayr

Dramatic Monologue

Mummy? Daddy? Is that you reading this?
Can you hear your lost son's whispering voice?
I write to you from Carrick Orphanage
I feel so lonely, deprived and frightened.
Mummy and Daddy, why did you leave me?
Where are you Mummy? Where are you Daddy?
I miss you so; my heart aches for you both!
None of the other children play with me
None of the other children care for me.
I sit here alone writing this,
Listening to the other children scream and shout.
They scream and shout with joy as they play together
They break my meagre things as they play their 'fun' games.
The wardens shout and hit me till I bleed
At night I cannot sleep, dreading the morn.
The days are long but the nights are longer.
I wish I was with you - my mum and dad.
I am sure you would treat me much better
School is hard but easier than Carrick.
The teachers like me so they do not beat me
I hate my life without you to look after me
Please come and get me, I miss you so much!

Rhona Ford (12)
Wellington School, Ayr

The Bat

Amidst the heavy shadows of the night
I skulk and lurk, then burst into flight
As I pass, people squeal and scream and squawk
And one even thought to hurl a rock.

Why do they hate me?
I'm not that bad
Why does the sight of me
Make them so mad?

I live in the darkness of a dark and murky cave
That no ordinary human would ever want to brave
I sleep in the day and fly in the night
I wallow in darkness and cower in light.

Why do they hate me?
I'm not that bad
Why does the sight of me
Make them so mad?

Leathery wings beat the air so fast
People see me for a second
And then I'm gone in a flash
Twirling and tumbling into the dark.

Why do they hate me?
I'm not that bad
Why does the sight of me
Make them so mad?

To people I am vermin
A horrible flying rat
But they never stop to think
That I'm just a bat.

Erin Corbett (12)
Wellington School, Ayr

Stonehenge

The mighty stones
The crown of a superpower
Power is held within these stones
The ruler of life
The writer of tales
Lord of all.

The mighty stones
Tall as tall can be
Giants piercing the solemn sky.

The crown of a superpower
A controller of men
Keeper of the peace.

Power is held within these stones
The lives of men
Their fates controlled.

The ruler of life
The maker of decisions
The court of ultimate justice.

Lord of all
Or so it was said
Entrusted with fate
Imbued in stone.

Robert Alner (13)
Wellington School, Ayr

My Favourite Place

When I feel down and upset
And I think the whole world is against me
I like to lie back and let the stress fly out of me
I head to my trampoline
My stress-remover machine
My wonderfully bouncy bed
My closest thing to flying
When I jump I think I am somewhere else
Bouncing on the fluffy clouds
With the wind rushing through my body
Then in space looking down on creation
Suddenly a mountain peak
My feet touching the freezing snow
Melting in-between my toes
But then I'm falling
Falling off a cliff face
I'm skydiving out of an aircraft about to hit the target
I hit the ground feet first
And I soar back up, the stress flooding out of me
Then I stop
Lie down and look up at the clouds
I see lots of animals roaming around
Their cloudy Animal Kingdom
Vehicles driving along the floating motorway
But before I know it, the stress has gone
I jump off, get my shoes on
And I enjoy a stress-free evening.

Oliver Greenall (12)
Wellington School, Ayr

The Japanese Mountain

The restful mountain sleeping silently
Cherry blossoms waving in the breeze
The sound of music drifts through the air
The mountain is waiting for something to happen.

In the heart of Japan the mountain rests
With the wind of magic blowing through the air
Charming you with its beauty
Waiting for the right time to show itself.

Through the window in the cherry blossom
The mountain lies peacefully waiting
Longing for the right time to come
But it could wake at any moment.

Mount Fuji rests for the time of just now
But obeys none but itself
But the wind is rising and the stones falling
And the mountain shall wake again.

Colin Casey (13)
Wellington School, Ayr

The White-Tipped Hills

Dreams take me there
My soul soars towards them
My heart is part of them
These are my hills.

They look down upon me
And at the wonders below
Some may be dark and stern
Others may be bright and peaceful
These are my hills.

They are rocks standing tall and firm
But they are also flowing empires
Of happiness and tranquillity
These are my hills.

The life of the hills
Generated by its centred heart
The heart that alights
Every emotion, every inch
Of growth, every spirit
These are my hills.

I, a mesmerised onlooker
Realise that those hills are too high
For even my dreams to reach
And this is true that those hills are still mine
And I am theirs . . .

Sophie Durnan (13)
Wellington School, Ayr

Dramatic Monologue

The war is on and I am useless to my men
Not knowing if I'll be here tomorrow
Or if they find me and I'm dying - or dead?
No food or water to keep me alive
But it doesn't matter to me if I die
As long as my people come out alive
Then so will I, but it means nothing to me
For me to live and my people to die
Then I will die here, alone, starved, dying - or dead?
And it will stay that way for as long as time goes on.

I hear gunshots, near, but not knowing where
Above ground, below ground, I just don't care
Maybe it's my slayers to set me at rest
I welcome them with open, yet distraught arms
I start thinking, supposing this, my final sight
This chamber that these men have put me in, with no water for weeks
This really could be the end; dying - or dead?
I prepare, but am not prepared for my decease
But a change of the wind, and I'll beat them to the job
I find a broken lance on the floor
I pick it up, stab myself and lie in the pool of blood
It's over and this time it's surely death.

Rónán Hunter Blair (12)
Wellington School, Ayr

Watching Angel

Don't cry! I'm here for you
Watching and waiting
Seeing and believing
I see your feelings
Feel the tears
I can hear your silent cries for help.

Don't fear! I'm here for you
I watch you stand
I see you looking for *me*
Looking for light
Yet looking at dark
I still hear your silent cries for help.

Don't worry! I'm here for you
I hear you breathe
Calming in the silence
Drifting into an endless mist
The trees close over, shut out the light
But I can still make out your cries for help.

Sleep! I'm here for you
The room is quiet
The night is glooming
Raindrops fall, land with a tap
Close your eyes, shut out your worries
Let your cries for help stop.

Ruth Dunsmuir (12)
Wellington School, Ayr

Alone

I wish I had . . .
I wish I could . . .
I wish I was anywhere but here.

I'm at school in the playground
Sitting all alone
Waiting for the school bell to ring
I feel like running home.

Everyone has a friend
Well, everyone but me
I tried to tell my mum and dad
But they don't care about me.

My life is like a storm
Blowing me away
Growing stronger by the minute
Life's too hard
Like a battle
I just can't win it.

I begin to cry
I just want to die
Just pass me the blade
I can't be saved
Heaven is calling for me
When I die my life will turn
To calm serenity.

Rachel Doyle (13)
Wellington School, Ayr

Beautiful

Beauty they say
Is in the eye of the beholder
But that eye can be twisted in time:
Beauty would be absent in change
Would that be beauty?
Not in your own mind.
Tell me dear beauty
What being are you?
Old and haggard?
Young, rich and fair?
What being is beauty?
Be what you dare.
Beauty be near me.
Don't ravage in time.
Beauty please hear me
O beauty sublime.
For what have I got?
At first glance I mean.
When everything fails me
Let beauty remain.
You are a curse
And a blessing the same.
You are beauty by name.
Yet where is the beauty
When tradition is gone?
Who says where it goes
And where it came from.
I tell you beauty is simply this:
If there is no beauty
There's no beautiful bliss.

Sarah Rowan
Wellington School, Ayr

My Sweet Jake

Lying down upon my bed, sweet eyes a-looking
Look at his eyes gazing
Brown and white, perfectly spotless
His brown eyes, large and puppy-like.

Even when my sweet Jake is dirty
His eyes are still as pretty
Out on a walk, he's jumping like a sweet kangaroo
He swims around in the river as graceful as a dolphin.

Every night when he's lying down on his bed
He reminds me of the day I got him, lying there in a ball
As once 'Upon A Time' he was vulnerable, curled up in that ball.

As he grows older, he's still as bouncy as could be
Now he's got a girlfriend, but down deep in my heart I know
                                                    he still loves me.

He lies there with this teddy Bluby (I think it's called)
I've sewn its ears 100 times before but that doesn't bother me
I'd do anything for Jake and he'd do anything for me
My springer spaniel, my sweet Jake.

Robyn Bonnar (12)
Whitburn Academy, Whitburn

Fairy In The Tree

I saw a fairy in the tree
And she was staring back at me
Lovely wings and golden glow
So I decided to put on a show
Then everybody came to see
The little fairy in the tree.

Alanna Rolland (12)
Whitburn Academy, Whitburn

Girl In A Wheelchair

In a wheelchair she sits
Bored to tears
Wants to stand
Wants to play
She can't do anything
As she sees children playing
She sits watching and
Waiting for spring.

Inside she feels so lonely and cold
She feels abandoned
She wants to be free
She wants to sing and dance
But she knows that will never happen.

But one thing she knows
Her family and friends are all around
So she's happy just to be here.

Danielle Hunter (12)
Whitburn Academy, Whitburn

Child Abuse

Reaching out to grab someone's hand to find that no one's there . . .
Waking up in the morning knowing that something bad will happen . . .
Being hurt in your own home for no reason . . .
Not knowing what's right from wrong . . .
Abandoned and all alone . . .
Having nightmares about your past . . .
Feeling that no one wants you and never will . . .
Too scared to speak out in case things get worse . . .
Wishing it would all go away, but most of the time
It never ends like it would in a fairy tale . . .

Dianne Hughes (13)
Whitburn Academy, Whitburn

Just A Tree

It was just a tree
The trunk was so beautiful and brown
It could put a smile on top of a frown.

It was very strong, sturdy and still
Looking at it was such a great thrill.

The leaves were all on the ground
I kicked them, they splashed and scattered around.

I climbed up this big tree
It was not very exciting, but an amazing adventure to me.

All around it was amazing, absolutely fine
I loved it to much, I wish it was all mine.

Although it was said to 'just be a tree'
Somehow it seemed much more to me.

Ryan Whyte (12)
Whitburn Academy, Whitburn

My Perfect Girl

She walks like a model
She dresses like a queen
She acts like a superstar
With teeth like a dentist.

She is as sexy as Katie Price
As hot as a chicken curry
As bright as the sun
With eyes like a star.

She is as beautiful as a flower
As sweet as a cake
As bright as a light bulb
That's my perfect girl.

Robbie Fairley (13)
Whitburn Academy, Whitburn

Young Writers Information

We hope you have enjoyed reading this book - and that you will continue to enjoy it in the coming years.

If you like reading and writing poetry drop us a line, or give us a call, and we'll send you a free information pack.

Alternatively if you would like to order further copies of this book or any of our other titles, then please give us a call or log onto our website at www.youngwriters.co.uk

**Young Writers Information
Remus House
Coltsfoot Drive
Peterborough
PE2 9JX**

(01733) 890066